PUB WALKS
IN NORTH

Forty Circular Walks

Around North Surrey Inns

John Quarendon

Other publications in the series
"Pub Walks in Dorset"
"Forty More Pub Walks in Dorset"
"Pub Walks in Somerset"
"Pub Walks in West Sussex"
"Pub Walks in East Sussex"
"Pub Walks in Devon"
"Pub Walks in Cornwall"
"Pub Walks in the New Forest"
"Pub Walks in Hardy's Wessex"
"Mike Power's Pub Walks Along the Dorset Coast"

1st edition published March 2001

Acknowledgements
Heart felt thanks to my wife Margaret, my constant walking companion
and to my daughter Suzy, who typed up all my scruffy notes

© John Quarendon

ISBN 1 898073 23 6

Power Publications
1 Clayford Ave
Ferndown, Dorset.
BH22 9PQ
www.powerpublications.co.uk

Printed by Pardy & Son (Printers) Ltd, Ringwood, Hants.
Front cover: The Four Horseshoes, Burrowhill.
Layout: Mike Power.
Photographs and drawings: John Quarendon.
2

Introduction

In 1999 I published a brief history of the Woking area combined with pub walks called "I'll Drink to That". This quickly sold out but, rather than reprint it with out of date pub information, Mike Power kindly invited me to expand the area, delete the historical notes and produce a book in his County Circular Pub Walks series. If you bought the earlier book, only thirteen of the twenty nine pubs featured therein are also included here and for the most part those walks have been altered substantially.

The Walks

The walks are circular, between 4 and 7 miles, and designed to start and finish at the featured pub. Where there are alternative free parking facilities en route I have shown these on the map as an aid to those who like to stop for lunch in the middle of a walk. The maps, drawn freehand, are generally in proportion but not precisely to scale. Distances quoted are in yards/miles as my legs are too short to pace in metres. As a small contribution to protecting the environment, where possible I have routed the walks past or close to the local railway station.

You can usually get away with summer walking in trainers but I strongly recommend walking boots at other times. Long trousers offer protection against nettles, brambles, ticks and biting insects. A walking stick is a useful aid in any encounter with nettles and brambles and, when raised, seems to act as a deterrent to over inquisitive cows. An Ordnance Survey, Explorer Series, 1:25000 map, a compass, Swiss army knife, antihistamine, bite/sting treatment, compact binoculars and compact camera are useful walking companions and should all fit into a decent sized bum bag.

The birdwatching notes in 'I'll Drink to That' were appreciated by some people so they are here again. They are restricted to the more unusual sightings or the book might have been twice as long.

The Pubs

The pubs have been selected primarily for their location related to the walks and, in this respect, several effectively chose themselves. Where a choice was possible the selection criteria were personal prejudice, particularly regarding choice of real ales and wines; appetising original menus with snacks and main meals and stressing the use of fresh ingredients and home cooking; value for money; low volume of any music; and separation of games, juke boxes, TVs and fruit machines from the dining area. Ambience is important and the sort of welcome you get when you walk up to the bar. A smile is good. It is sensible to book in advance for parties of ten or more (less on Sundays). Please ask permission before parking to walk.

Pubs are constantly changing hands, changing character or being closed down. If what you find here is not what you find there, you will know that another one has bitten the dust in the interval between the writing and the walking.

The Country Code

This paragraph appears in some form in all walking guides. Please keep to footpaths, shut all gates, damage no property, light no fires, dig no bulbs, leave no litter and keep dogs on leads near livestock. Kiss at all kissing gates if suitably accompanied. If not hang about for the U3A party coming along behind. Somebody's granny/grandad might make your day.

NORTH WEST SURREY

MAP OF WALK LOCATIONS

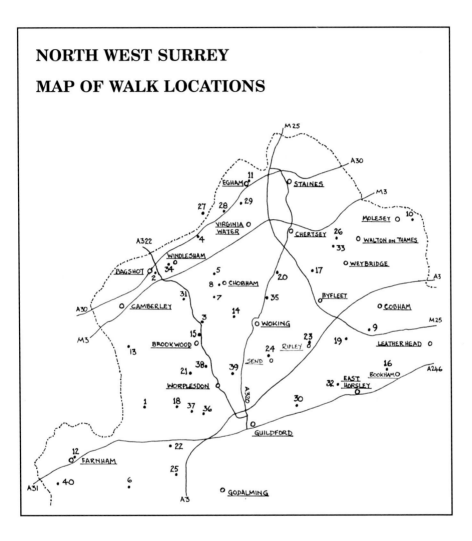

The Nightingale, Ash

There are three pubs within a couple of hundred yards on the Normandy side of Ash. No disrespect to the other two but I would probably have been drummed out of the RSPB if I had not called first at the Nightingale. No need to look further. Three pumps dispensing Hog's Back Brewery's TEA, Hop Garden Gold and Nightingale, a specially commissioned blend of Hop Garden Gold and Hair of the Hog, which at 4.0 ABV is certainly worth trilling about.

Martin Doherty, the owner of this smart little Free House since November 1999, has certainly hit on a winning formula of the finest ales and good home cooked English pub grub at sensible prices. No gimmicks, what you see is what you get. The standard menu covers a good choice of salads, jackets, ploughmans and sandwiches and the backboard lists a daily choice of starters and puddings and a good range of main courses such as lamb casserole, pork chop, game pie, beef and Guinness pie, grilled trout, etc.

The pub is open from 11am to 2.30pm and 6-11pm daily, with lunch served from 12 to 2pm and dinner from 6-9pm. Children are welcome in the pub and dogs in the garden only. NB. The pub does not accept bookings so, on Sundays particularly, the advice is to come early to avoid disappointment.

Telephone: 01252 326079.

The pub is situated on the A323 to the east of Ash, about 500 yards from Ash station.

Approx. distance of walk: 4 miles. Start at OS Map Ref. SU 905512.

There is ample parking behind the pub. To pick up the walk from Ash Station, turn left over the level crossing and in a few yards turn right at a fingerpost. Pass through a lovely meadow with much wildlife – butterflies, goldfinches, yellow hammers, and a kestrel. At a fork keep ahead, cross a road and pass a scout hut to join the walk at the novel white painted *pinch stile (para 1).

A walk across farmland frequented by deer in Normandy and Wyke, followed by an airy stretch amid pine woods on Normandy Common, where there may be wet areas.

1 Cross the road from the pub and turn right, then left through a barrier into a sports field. Bear left at the bottom corner and turn left on a path through a *pinch style. Maintain direction on a path between fields and over a farm drive. At a road turn right then left into Wyke Ave. At the end turn right on a footpath behind a wire fence. Where the path becomes a track turn left through a gap in trees and across the middle of a field. At the next field bear right and then along the field edge. Deer are frequently to be seen on the other side of the field. Cross two stiles and go diagonally across the field (or left handed round the edge if there is a crop). Cross a stile, then a footbridge and at an immediate fork keep left. Join a grassy

path between fences and at the end go left beside gardens.
2 Turn left at a road and right into the churchyard of Wyke church. The churchyard has been designated a site of Natural Conservation Interest. Cross diagonally to the other gate and turn right down the road. Opposite the Vicarage turn left at a fingerpost. Go over footbridges and steadily uphill ignoring side paths to reach a sports field. Bear left around the pitch and before you reach the pavilion cross a drive that leads to a car park and bear left into woodland at a bridleway waymark. Ignore the stile ahead. The path bends right and at a fork keep right uphill aided by steps. Cross a road and go ahead on a track beside 'Hillside'. At

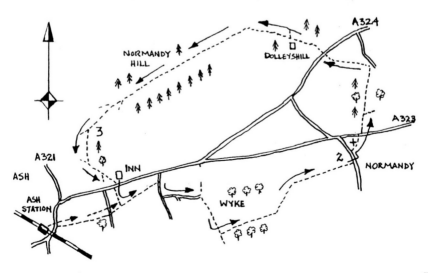

Walk No. 1

Dolley's Hill Park go ahead past a barrier on a grassy path. In 75 yards go over a crossing path. The path wends up hill with a fence on the left. There may be wet patches but there is usually a way round them. At the top of a rise bear half right across a track and down to a military 'No Entry' sign. Turn left along the fence and keep to this path, which gives you fine views across the heather clad hills. (Route finding through the woods is just too complicated.) There may be wet patches here too but they may easily be circumvented by slipping between the wires of the MOD fence unless the red flags are flying.

3 Continue to the top of a very steep rise (there is a seat at the top) and go on another 100 yards or so to a flagpole. Turn left here, go over a crossing track and past a clearing with a seat on the left. Where the track bends right by another seat go ahead on a path that goes steeply down hill into woodland. Go over a crossing path and at the next wider crossing path turn left and immediately fork right downhill. At the next fork keep left back to the pub.

Kestrel taking a dust bath

The White Hart, Bagshot

People often ask in a place with several pubs how the selection is made for the walk. In this case why walk past four other pubs to get to Church Road, the effective start of the walk? Briefly, on the Sunday lunchtime we visited one had no real ale only the frothy, freezing, 'smooth' variety; one had three screens tuned to Sky Sport and no food; one had three pumps all dispensing Courage Best with no alternative and we were warned off the fourth by two locals who said it was "full of outsider riff-raff who had been banned from their own neighbourhood pubs!" All my prejudices apart from loud pop music catered for, so on to the White Hart, a Unique Pub Company (Courage empire) establishment. Leo Farnon took over as licensee in May 2000. He quickly redecorated externally, installed a chef and introduced a sensibly priced, appetising and imaginative new menu. The external impression is of a tiny pub but it is big enough inside with a family room/conservatory to the side and a very well equipped beer garden at the rear with children's playground, basketball and an aviary. There is a decent wine list and ales regularly available are Young's Special, Marston's Pedigree, Brakspear's and Courage Best, plus a guest. Blackboard specials include the likes of red snapper salad, rainbow trout on a bed of tagliatelle with Mediterranean seared vegetables and chicken Madras on pilau rice with onion and tomato salad in a puppodum basket with naan bread. Leo says he expects to complete the transformation with an interior refurbishment early in 2001.

Dogs on a lead are welcome in the pub and garden.

The pub is open all day seven days a week with lunchtime food served from 12-2.30pm.

Telephone: 01276 473640.

Walk No. 2

The pub is situated in Guildford Road Bagshot ¼ mile east of the A30.

Approx. distance of walk: 5 miles. Start at OS Map Ref. SU 915633.

There is limited parking at the pub but plenty of room in the free car park behind the Somerfield supermarket in The Square – see map. The start point is ¼ mile from Bagshot railway station.

This is an exercise walk for the striders with only two kissing gates, one pseudo stile and a couple of short sharp hills to slow you down. The route is on long straight paths through woodland and over heathland where highwaymen once roamed. Nowadays most of the riders you meet will be on mountain bikes and you are unlikely to see another walker.

1 Turn right out of the pub, pass under the railway arch and at the roundabout go left up the High Street to the A30. Turn left, cross the road at the lights then go right and left into Church Road. Pass the rather elegant St Anne's Church and continue gently uphill as the road changes its name to College Ride. Go through a kissing gate and later beside a barrier and beneath sweet chestnut trees. At the top of Penny Hill fork left to go over a crossing track and beneath power lines. Pass a waymark post on your right and bear right over a crossing path to reach a school fence.
2 Turn right along the fence and maintain direction as the path widens to cross under the power lines again. Ignore side turnings and the path narrows to reach a car park with an aerial mast to the right. Cross a

ditch and bear half right across the car park to go beside a metal barrier onto a wide track. After 30 yards at a waymark post fork left into woodland. Every hollow holds a puddle along here but there is plenty of room to pass at the sides. Cross a wide track and continue ahead on a gravel track through heather and young pine trees. Go over a crossing track and at a fork go right steeply down hill into woodland. Keep ahead where three tracks converge and in 75 yards, just before another major junction of tracks, turn right over a wooden barrier. Immediately at a fork bear right. Your way is up the sandy hill ahead, which proves to be just the start of a switchback course where, if you walk in the middle of the track, you will have your left foot in Berkshire and your right foot in Surrey.

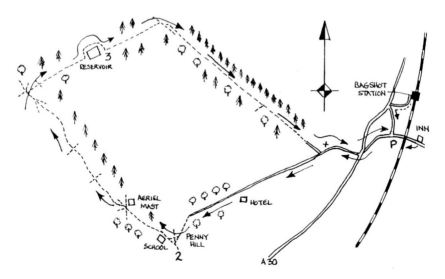

3 At a fence before the reservoir on top of Surrey Hill turn left and follow the perimeter fence round to the gate on the other side. With your back to the gate go straight ahead soon steeply downhill. Go over a crossing track and at a 'T' junction turn right. After 50 yards bear left to a kissing gate beside a metal gate and go ahead on a path between fences. Stay on this path for one mile towards the end of which it becomes a residential road. At a 'T' junction turn left into Church Road and retrace your steps back to the pub.

"There are a couple of pubs named after me in here somewhere"

The Fox, Bisley

For a walker the Fox is ideally situated. Easy to find on the A322 Guildford to Bagshot road, it is beside the footpath to Bisley Church and opposite the entrance to Bisley Common. From the outside it is not a pretty pub, although the inn sign is charming enough. Inside, however, there is evidence of its 200 year history with exposed beams and a wooden arch. The front section of the pub divides nicely into alcoves and a games section with dart board and machines. Tables in the side extension overlook the patio and garden and there is a pleasant separate dining room. Gas fires add to the winter cheer.

Alan and Valerie Sparkes retired in October 2000 after 14 years at the Fox and new licensee, 'Greg' Gregorian has installed a new chef and simplified the menu. Main courses include salmon in beer batter, as a change from the endangered cod, chargrilled tuna salad and smoked haddock, lentil and asparagus tart. They specialise in exotic sandwiches in a choice of white, wholemeal or ciabatta bread, all served with salad dressing and crisps. Examples are chargrilled rib-eye steak with pepper and horseradish cream and mozzarella with plum tomato, avocado and black pepper.

Also on offer as before are Courage Directors and Best. Children are welcome. Dogs in the garden on a lead only, please.

The pub is open from 11am-3pm and 5-11pm Monday to Thursday and all day Fridays and weekends. Lunchtime food is served from 12-2pm.

Telephone: 01483 473175.

The pub is situated on the A322 Guildford to Bagshot road south of Bisley.

Approx. distance of walk: 4½ miles. Start at OS Map Ref. SU 955589.

Parking is in front of the pub.

This is a circular tour of Bisley on leafy lanes passing the ancient church and the shooting ranges and concluding across Bisley Common. There may be mud towards the end.

1 From the pub turn left and at the bus stop left again past a gate onto a track. After about half a mile down this shady lane turn left over a battered stile into a field. Little owls nest near here. Make your way along the right hand edge of the field to a kissing gate into Bisley Churchyard. Note the wooden spire with cedar shingles and the traditional yew tree by the ancient porch. The church is not usually open and there is no

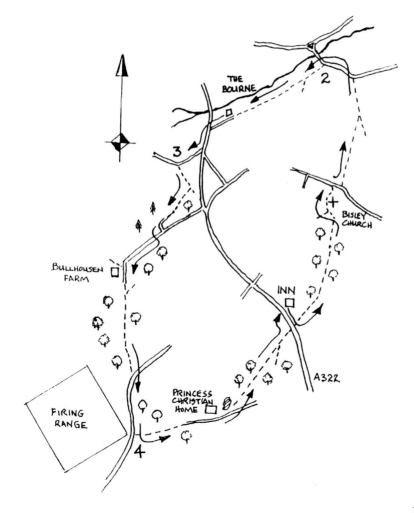

13

Walk No. 3

information on how to obtain a key. Leave the church by the drive, turn right on the road and after a few yards left over a stile. Follow the right hand edge of the field, cross a stile and continue onto the edge of a golf course. Cross one footbridge and bear right, then another by the 6th tee sign where you go left on a narrow tree lined path. Go over a crossing path and immediately fork left to reach Beldam Bridge Road where you turn left.

2 Seventy five yards before the bridge turn left at a bridleway fingerpost. At a fork keep right on the bridleway and ignore a stile on the left. The path widens to a track which may be wet initially and pheasants may start up before you. Reach an industrial site and bear left on a metalled road. Turn left at the A322 and soon right into Ford Road.

3 Where the road bends right go left at a fingerpost past a lily pond. Where the path bends round 'Cornerways' bear right on a grass path. Cross the drive to Lincluden Nursery and maintain direction on a narrow path into woodland. At a fingerpost turn right on a lane past houses then first left. At a 'T' junction turn right. Continue down this lane and bear left past the entrance to Bullhousen Farm. At a fork by a finger post go right on the narrower path, then immediately at the next fork go left. At a fingerpost keep ahead and at a fork go left. Go over a crossing path and at a 'T' junction turn right to meet an unmade road where you turn left. Follow this road as it bends left and right to reach Queens Road where you turn right.

4 After about 300 yards, with a firing range on your right, turn left on an unmade road at a fingerpost. At a fork go right into woods and then join a track. At a 'T' junction go left on a road signed Bridleway No 144. Pass the Princess Christian Homes for disabled servicemen and Stafford Lake and then go left at a fingerpost on muddy Bridleway No 143. Cross a farm drive and at a fork keep left. At a junction of three paths take the left hand one to cross a farm drive by a small pond. This is literally alive with frogs in the mating season. At a junction of paths maintain direction with a fence on your left. At the end of the fence by Snowdrop Farm keep ahead on a drive to reach the A322. Cross over and turn left back to the pub.

Bisley church

The Broomhall Hutt, Broomhall

The Sunningdale Golf course nearby has a half way refreshment hut and the Broomhall Hutt carries that concept beyond the 18th hole. The pub and the menu have a golfing theme and caddies are among the regulars, hence the appearance on the menu of the 'Broomhall Platter', really a big breakfast. First in at lunchtime are the regular wrinklies seeking easy to chew options like the chef's home made cottage pie. The menu is wide ranging including a range of omelettes, jacket potatoes, with a choice of ten fillings, five salads and three vegetarian dishes all reasonably priced. Unusually for a freehouse the ale on offer is limited to Courage Best and Directors with no guests. The evening clientele are mostly the young set and they are catered for with three draft lagers.

Privately owned by Joan Vincent-Fernie for 10 years, the pub is a friendly local with a dining area one side of the bar and a pool table the other. There is a small courtyard garden at the rear.

The pub is open all day every day. Lunchtime food is served from 12-2pm.

Dogs are welcome and children in the dining area.

Telephone: 01344 876887.

Walk No. 4

The pub is situated on the A30 just to the east of Sunningdale Railway Station.

Approx. distance of walk: 6 miles. Start at OS Map Ref. SU 955669.

Parking is available behind the pub or at Chobham Place Woods – see map.

With the demise of The Cricketers at Burrow Hill the Broomhall Hutt is now the nearest hostelry to the northern section of Chobham Common. This results in some unavoidable repetition at the beginning and end of the walk, which circles the common and also visits Chobham Place Woods and the monument to Queen Victoria. The walk offers good opportunities for bird watchers – look out particularly for hobby falcons, stonechats, meadow pipits and Dartford warblers and many species of dragonfly and butterfly. The walk is mostly on bridle paths for ease of route finding and so may be muddy after rain.

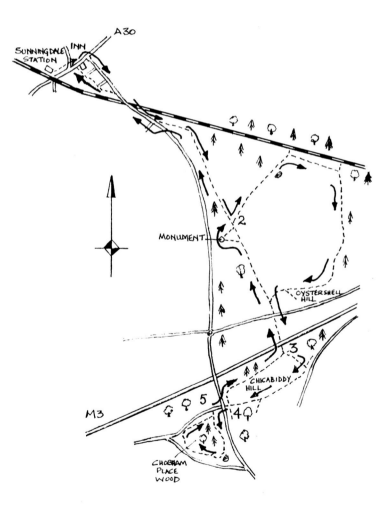

1 Turn right out of the pub and right again into Chobham Road. Cross a railway bridge and just past Richmond Wood on the right cross the road to enter Chobham Common at a signpost. Follow this undulating track for over half a mile to reach a crossing track at the top of a rise where you turn sharp left.

2 Follow this bridle path across the common. At a fork by a waymarked post keep left. At a fork go right on the narrower path to pass a pond and rejoin the main track. Keep left on the main track at a waymark post and again at the next one and ignore a right fork. The track bends left to a gate before the railway. Turn right here and at the next crossing track adjacent to the railway turn right on the bridleway. Keep to this main bridleway following the waymarks. Pass Oystershell Hill on your left (or climb it for the view) and the path curves right down to a crossing track, where you turn left to pass under the M3 via a subway.

3 At a fork go left and at the next fork right. At a 'T' junction before a road turn right. Pass Chicabiddy Hill on your right, resplendent in purple heather in July, and go over a crossing track at a marker post. Reach a crossing track before a road.

4 Cross into Valley End Road and after 100 yards turn left into the car park for Chobham Place Woods, which are worth a circular walk of their own. (However if you are pushed for time you can go straight to paragraph 5 and save the pleasure for another day). Go into the woods to the right of the notice board and head down the avenue of pine trees. After about 80 yards go left on a narrow path. Note the small Crimean War memorial on the left under rhododendrons. At a 'T' junction turn right and at two forks keep right on the wider path. At the next two forks in quick succession keep left. Reach a pond on your left and then turn right across the avenue of trees you started in. The path bends left and then right to reach a road. Just before the road take the path which bears half right across a raised land boundary into the woods. This path runs roughly parallel to the road and takes you back to the car park. Turn right along Valley End Road, cross the main road and retrace your steps to the waymark posts just inside the common.

5 At the waymark posts turn left following the sign 'Horse ride no cycles'. For the avoidance of doubt, if you have missed out para 4 the road should now be on your left. The path bends right through gorse and at a junction of paths keep ahead. At a fork go left and left again back through the subway under the M3. At the other side keep ahead on the sandy bridleway you were on earlier. Cross the road and keep ahead past a barrier and again at a waymarked crossing of bridleways. Pass two waymarked posts and go uphill to another where you turn left. Ahead is the granite monument to Queen Victoria, which can be reached by a short diversion from the path.

6 Return to the bridleway and immediately at another waymark go left down hill. You are now on the path on which you first entered the common. Retrace your steps to the Chobham Road and turn right over the railway bridge. Immediately on the other side turn left on a signed footpath. Cross a gravel drive and then a road and at the next 'T' junction opposite 'Halfpenny House' turn left down to the A30 and right back to the Broomhall Hutt.

Queen Victoria Monument

17

The Four Horseshoes, Burrowhill

At 9 o'clock in the morning the Four Horseshoes is a picture. Set back from Burrowhill Green with a shady yew tree to the left and smothered in hanging baskets it looks the perfect village pub. Later the view is spoiled by parked cars but inside the same village atmosphere prevails with low beams and a farming and horsey theme to the decoration. The one jarring note is a West Ham United mirror in the lounge bar – possibly donated by Trevor Brooking to annoy Gary Lineker, who is a customer here? The pub is always busy, the more so since the demise of the Cricketers, now an Italian restaurant.

The pub is owned by Eldridge Pope, another part of the Courage Empire, but landlord John Andrews offers Charles Wells' Bombardier and Brakspear's Bitter as alternatives to the Courage Best.

The 'specials' blackboard has been taken over for the extensive wine list including nine sold by the glass.

The specials now appear on a daily printed sheet and include chillies and curries and such as garlic chicken breast.

Aside from the lounge bar there is a Snug, which is ideal for a family, and a separate dining room.

The pub is open from 11am-3pm and 5.30-11pm, Monday to Saturday and 12-3pm and 7-10.30pm Sundays. Food is served from 12-2pm and 7-9.30-pm.

Telephone: 01276 857581.

The pub is situated at Burrowhill Green, ¾ mile north of Chobham village centre on the B383.

Approx. distance of walk: 4 miles. Start at OS Map Ref. SU 970629.

There is a car park behind the pub and also space at the roadside.

Several walks have been published covering the southern section of Chobham Common. For ease of route finding they tend to follow the perimeter but this involves walking in woodland most of the time, which misses the essential character of the heath and its wildlife. This route has been selected to find the wildlife particularly the birds, and to enjoy the views. In summer birdwatchers look out for Dartford warblers, stonechats, hobby falcons and nightingales. As there are not many obvious reference points en route I have inserted the row of pylons on the map. If you get lost follow their line from north east to south west and that will put you back on track.

1 With your back to the pub, walk to the inn sign and turn left. Cross the road into Gorse Lane and turn left into Heather Way. At a crossing track bear right round the telegraph pole then left at a waymark into woodland. At a field gate turn left and after 30 yards turn right on a path that runs parallel to the field edge. Go ahead over a crossing track at a waymarked barrier and cross a lane to the entrance to Jubilee Mount. Duck

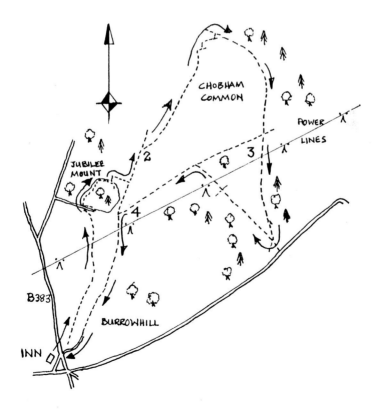

Walk No. 5

under the barrier and bear left along the fence. There are supposed to be nightingales in this little reserve but a family of five green woodpeckers simply laughed at the idea as they scattered before us. Pass a stile and a seat and the path bends right. There is a nice view from the next seat. Just before the path bends right again leave the enclosure by turning left between wooden railings. Turn right on the track, pass a waymark post and at a waymarked junction of paths turn left on the gravel track. A vista across the heath now opens up and stonechats pose on the tops of gorse and birch and remark upon our passing.

2 At a fork bear right off the gravel track and then over a crossing track. Pass waymark post No.4. At a fork keep left on the wider track. The path begins to bear left and at a crossing track by waymark post No.5 turn right. At a fork turn left on a narrow path that goes up steeply to the hilltop. Three are seats here from which to enjoy the views. With your back to the seats take the narrow path at 1 o'clock, go over the crossing track and continue across the heather. At a fork go left on an equally narrow path and turn right on a crossing track. The track bends right and goes steeply down hill with the aid of steps. Having scanned the trees to the left with binoculars in vain for the hobby falcons one 'buzzed' us as we were going down these steps. At a fork keep right and go over a wide crossing track and under power lines.

3 Go over a waymarked crossing path and, in 70 yards, join a wider path and keep ahead. After 300 yards pass to the right of a waymark post and at the next wide crossing track turn sharp right. This track goes gently uphill for ¼ mile then down over a waymarked crossing path with a pylon up to the right. Continue ahead soon uphill in soft sand under the power lines again. The Dartford warbler appeared on cue here and treated us to several snatches of scratchy song from the lower branches of a birch sapling. Three out of four is not bad. The path descends to a wide crossing path where you turn left. Keep on this track running roughly parallel to the power lines.

4 Pass a seat on your right and go downhill to a point with waymark posts on both sides of the track and turn left. Pass under the power lines, ignore side paths and go over a crossing track by a waymark post. At the next crossing track with a waymark post 15 yards to your right go straight ahead through pine trees and turn right on Gorse Lane back to the pub.

Stonechat

Hobby

The Donkey, Charles Hill

The Donkey dates from 1730 and there is an interesting potted history on the wall in the conservatory. It features regularly in the Good Pub Guide and so it should. In fact it is difficult to avoid gibbering superlatives about every facet of this lovely pub. The oak beams, the horsey pictures, the brasses and copper utensils, the fresh flowers, the interesting chairs. There is a smart dining area and conservatory and a patio with Champagne umbrellas. Everything sparkles including the service in this Greene King pub. Abbot, IPA and Old Speckled Hen are the resident ales and the menu caters for all tastes from hungry walkers to the Ladies Who Lunch. There are sandwiches plain, toasted and club, assorted jackets, ham and eggs, Cumberland sausages, and 'Donkey' salads in variety. The L.W.L are catered for with an extraordinary choice including lobster thermidor, breast of guinea fowl, corn fed chicken breast with scallops and oriental chicken with stuffed mango rolled in coconut. The prices are commensurate with the quality, the plates are large and the portions generous, with smaller portions pro rata for children in addition to the special children's menu.

Dogs are welcome and walkers are politely requested to remove muddy boots before entering. And the donkey? There are now two, 'Pip' and 'Dusty'.

The pub is open Monday to Saturday from 11am-2.30pm and 6-11pm. Food is served from 12-2pm and 6.30-9.30pm. On Sunday lunch is served from 12-2.15pm and the kitchen is closed Sunday evening.

Telephone: 01252 702124.

Walk No. 6

The pub is situated at Charles Hill on the B3001 Farnham to Milford road, west of Elstead.

Approx. distance of walk: 5½ miles. Start at OS Map Ref. SU 893444.

The roof of the pub is below the level of the B3001 and the steep drive down to the car park is easily missed. Look out for the inn sign at road level. There is a free public car park at Tilford Green by the bridge and a small one outside the Waverley Abbey grounds.

This is a favourite walk. The Waverley Abbey ruin is in a lovely setting by the River Wey and other attractions include the much filmed Tilford Village Green, with its ancient oak and bridge and the heather of Crooksbury Common. There is no mud to speak of even on the bridle paths.

1 Leave the pub up the drive, cross the road and bear left on a signed bridleway. At a fork keep left uphill past 'Firbank' and maintain direction into Crooksbury Wood. Plod uphill

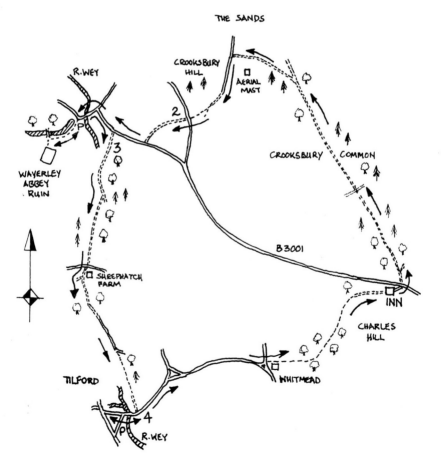

in the soft sand and admire the heather. Ignore side paths and continue ahead past the next barrier. At a fingerpost past 'Longlands' fork left and turn left on a road. The road becomes a track, a long way from the sea but known as Smugglers Way, and at a bridleway waymark fork right on a path. In twenty yards at a fork keep left and left again at post 581. Continue downhill to a road passing two more 581 posts.

2 Cross to a finger post by 'Waverley Cottage' and continue on the bridleway. Turn right on a road past Keeper's Cottage Stud. At Waverley Lane turn left, cross the bridge over the R. Wey and turn left at the entrance to Waverley Abbey House. To visit the ruins go through the car park and the kissing gate. In season you will probably see swallows, sand and house martins, grey wagtails and herons on the stretch of river up to the bridge. Retrace your steps to the road and over the bridge and turn right on the B3001 towards Godalming.

3 In about 200 yards turn right at a fingerpost with a red arrow. At a fingerpost turn right on a Public Byway uphill. Cross a road to a fingerpost and turn right up a track. Fork left past Sheephatch Farm and at a waymark post follow the red arrow left. Join a lane and note the unusual elevated beech hedge on the left. Opposite 'Wey Cottage' fork right at a fingerpost. Ignore paths to the left and turn right on a road to visit the picturesque Tilford Green.

4 Retrace your steps over the bridge and up the road and continue to turn right into Whitmead Lane. Ignore unusual left turn and stay on this quiet lane for half a mile. Where the lane bends sharp left go ahead at a fingerpost to the left of 'Whitmead' and continue back to the pub.

Mediaeval Bridge over the River Wey, Tilford

The Castle Grove, Chobham

The Castle Grove was built in the 1850's as a station for a railway line that eventually took another route. The front entrance is the original divided saloon door style popular at the time, although the two sides have now been joined to open on one side only. A nice feature is that the paintings round the walls are for sale so the décor frequently changes. Most pubs these days seem to be permanently advertising for staff. Brian and Jenny Pemble must be doing something right because in this local the same friendly staff are always there and the customers keep coming back. The food never disappoints, honey roast ham and home made curries being particular favourites with 'Spotted Richard' pudding to follow. The menu is extensive e.g. there are eight salads to choose from and there is a daily specials board.

Ales on tap usually include Young's Special, Charles Wells' Bombadier, Greene King IPA and a guest.

The garden is well equipped for youngsters with a bouncy train a permanent summer feature. Indoors children and dogs are welcome in the public bar.

The pub is open Monday to Thursday 11am-2.30pm, Friday 11am-3pm, Saturday 11am-3.30pm and Sunday 12-3pm. Evenings from 5.30-11pm, Sunday 7-10.30pm. Food is served from 12-2pm and, on Thursday to Saturday only, from 6.30-9pm. The kitchen is closed on the other evenings.

Telephone: 01276 858196.

Walk No. 7

The pub is situated half a mile south of Chobham village in Castle Grove Road.

Approx. distance of walk: 4½ miles. Start at OS Map Ref. SU 971611.

There is ample parking at the pub.

A varied walk through woodland, across farmland and along a river bank teeming with birdlife, finishing through Chobham village past the church of St Lawrence. A walking stick may be useful to deal with nettles early on.

1 From the front of the pub cross to the pavement and turn left up Castle Grove Road towards the village, then right down Broadford Lane. Continue along this lane to the end where you turn left still on Bridleway No 14. Cross the Bourne over a footbridge. The path eventually widens into a gravel road and you continue to the A3046 Woking road. Turn right for 150 yards and just past a drive go right into woodland at a waymark post. The next two waymark posts have been pulled up but it does not present a problem. At a fork take the more pronounced path to the left curving away from the field edge and at a gravel road go left past a sign for Footpath No 117. At a wooden fence turn right down the drive to Milford Farm. Pass entrance gates and just before a garage go beside the wooden fence down the side of the garage and then a house. This footpath, No 116, is fine in April but by September it can become overgrown with nettles and brambles. Enter Daydawn Nursery and turn right on a track for a few yards and then left over a stile and left again. Immediately at a fork keep right between a leylandii hedge and a water tank. At the end of the hedge go half right to a stile by a gate and out to an unmade road where you turn left. After 150 yards go right on Footpath No 120. At a waymarked post keep left on the narrower path which reaches a road via a footbridge. Turn right and after 150 yards cross the road and turn down a signed footpath.

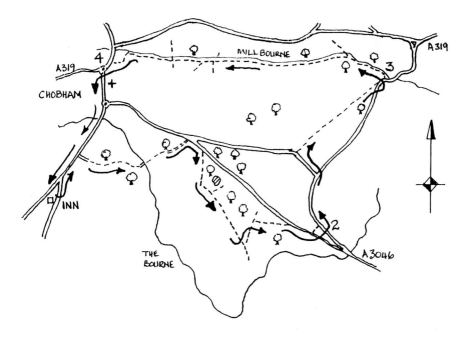

25

2 Reach Philpot Lane, turn left and later left again into Sandpit Hall Road. Just before Trotters Lane turn right over a stile into a field. Keep to the left-hand edge of two fields then maintain direction on an enclosed path past back gardens. This may become overgrown in summer, another use for that walking stick. Cross a stile into a field and head for another stile beside a white gate. Continue to the bottom right hand corner of the next field and out to Philpot Lane again. Turn left and in 75 yards left again on a signed footpath.

3 Cross a footbridge and join the footpath beside the Mill Bourne. This can be a rewarding stretch for bird watchers. Look out for kingfishers, kestrels, goldfinches and whitethroats among others. In summer the banks are lined with Indian balsam up to 6 feet high. Stay on this path with the river on your right for just over a mile. At the end follow the path left for 40 yards and turn right on a path between fences.

4 Cross a car park entrance to reach a road and turn left through Chobham village. Pass the picturesque Cannon Corner and bear left at the roundabout. The church of St Lawrence dates from 1080 and retains some original Norman features. Massive chalk columns dating from the 12th century, a chest dated 1250, eight bells the oldest of which dates from 1520 and a rare octagonal wooden font of the same vintage are all of interest. Continue from the church and keep right at the next roundabout back to the Castle Grove.

Cannon Corner

The Sun, Chobham

Following the demise of the historic White Hart opposite, now an 'eating house', the redoubtable villagers of Chobham put up a fight when a similar fate threatened the Sun. Several of them clubbed together to purchase this 16th century Grade II listed pub and it is now managed on their behalf. The ambience is friendly but sophisticated with it, two fires in winter and old beams strewn with hop vines. The lounge bar that leads to the separate restaurant at the rear has window seats and copper topped circular tables. The public bar is similar without the copper and there is a central area with a shelf and bar stools in front of a bay window. Ales are Pedigree, Courage Best and Directors and the excellent Ringwood's Best.

The menu is a revelation far removed from those chain pubs where you can have egg, sausage and chips because there is a button on the till for it but not sausage, chips and beans because 'we can't put it into the automated till'. Here the chef will be pleased to try to accommodate customers' special requirements. There is a choice of 6 ploughman's and 16 sandwiches and chef will make you a salad from any of the sandwich ingredients; and you can specify the temperature of your curry from candle to furnace. The choice of 10 jacket potato fillings includes hoi sin duck and among other delights are stir fried chicken and prawns and prawn linguini in tomatoes and pernod. This is a pub where even while you are savouring your own meal you find yourself gazing enviously at the other appetising dishes emanating from the kitchen. Excellent and a certain recommendation for the Good Pub Guide.

Children are only allowed in the restaurant and dogs not at all. There are a few tables outside but no garden.

Opening hours are 11am-3pm and 5.30-11pm on six days and 12-3pm and 7-10.30pm on Sundays. Food is served from 12-2.30 and 7.30-9.30pm but not on Sunday or Monday evenings.

Telephone: 01276 857112.

Walk No. 8

The pub is situated in Chobham High Street.

Approx. distance of walk: 4½ miles. Start at OS Map Ref. SU 973617.

There is some parking at the pub or in the free car park 200 yards north – see map.

A walk on little used paths and lanes over farmland and nursery land to the west of Chobham village. Section 3-4 passes through fields in which horses are usually grazing and there may be muddy patches where they congregate. A walking stick might be useful to tame nettles in the same section.

1 Turn left out of the pub. (The Church of St Lawrence opposite is well worth a visit – see **Walk 7, para 4**.) After 20 yards turn left onto Footpath No.17 and in another 20 yards go right past a school. At a road cross over, turn left then right down the drive to 'Town Mill'. Go right then left around an office building to join an enclosed footpath beside a drive. Cross a footbridge and at a road turn left. Turn left into Leslie Road and after 100 yards turn right on Footpath No.47. Where the grassy path enters a field keep to the right of a barbed wire fence. Go through a kissing gate and bear right away from the fence. Pass a wooden gate to reach a nursery road. Cross to a stile and maintain direction over another. At a wooden fence turn right and continue with a hedge on your left as far as a wooden gate in the hedge. Go through and turn right on farm drive. Turn right on a road, then after 15 yards go left over a stile. At the next stile and fingerpost turn right and shortly cross a stile and turn left along a fence. Cross another stile to join a farm drive by stables. Pause to admire some attractive property before reaching a road where you turn left.

2 Continue along this usually quiet road for about half a mile. At the top of a rise at a fingerpost turn left on a path. Go down hill between fields and through a kissing gate to a road. Cross and turn right making use of

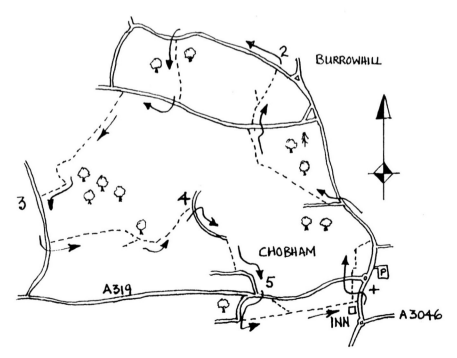

28

the grass verge as necessary. Pass Dingley Dell Nurseries and at a fingerpost turn left on a grassy path. Turn left over a footbridge into the nursery and immediately right down the side of a field. Keep ahead on a concrete road. Where the concrete bends left go forward to cross a footbridge into a polo field. A fingerpost invites you to cross the polo field 'in single file' or to go left around the edge. Choose one according to circumstances at the time and arrive at a waymarked footbridge over Clapper's Brook. Cross into another polo field and follow the direction of a waymark half left to the corner of a line of trees. Just before the corner go left on a waymarked path which goes just inside the woodland over a stile and then bends right to go between fences to reach Halebourne Lane.

3 Turn left, pass Higher Park Farm and go left through the gate of Roebuck Farm. There is a stile just past the gate but it leads into an enclosed area. It may be worth having a peep over the stile to see some 'mop headed' chickens and other rare breeds in pens. From the gate go ahead to a stile beside a metal gate and then another. Go half right to a stile in the middle of a field and maintain direction to a stile in the bottom corner of the next field. You may have to negotiate nettles and a fallen tree here before making your way along the right hand edge of the field with a stream on your right. Pass a footbridge and head through a gap in bushes then diagonally across a field towards a corrugated iron barn. Exit over a metal barrier beside the gate, congratulate yourself on passing the route finding exam and bear left on a grass path between fields.

4 At a lane turn right. Where the lane ends or, strictly speaking, bends right and becomes a stream in wet weather, cross a waymarked stile and turn right on a path. Negotiate a stile then a footbridge beside a ford and turn left into Clappers Lane. Spotted flycatchers nested by the listed 'Bournebrook Cottage' in 1999 and 2000 but the dog may object if you stand watching them for too long.

5 Reach the busy A319 Bagshot Road, turn right for a few yards then left down Pennypot Lane. Where the road bends sharp right by 'Pennypot Cottage' go left over a stile into a field. Keep beside the left hand fence to cross two more stiles and then maintain direction on a path between a hedge and a fence. Continue on this path through nursery land and past the cemetery to Chobham High Street, where turn right back to the pub.

Church of St Lawrence

The Cricketers, Downside

This centuries old Inntrepreneur inn, run by Brian and Wendy Luxford, must be one of the most popular pubs in Surrey. It features regularly in the Good Pub Guide and its authentic 'olde worlde' charm makes it a very attractive venue. The old timbers are enhanced by a large collection of horse brasses, brass salvers and other ornaments. There are solid oak tables with fresh flowers, barrel stools and a fine working fireplace.

Sherry is served from casks behind the bar. Ales regularly available are Old Speckled Hen, 6X and Theakston's and Young's bitters and there are nine wines available by the glass. The pub is always busy and the advice is to come early.

The menu is on blackboards above the separate food counter and in summer offers an astonishing selection of 28 salads, including dressed crab, rollmops, poached trout and gala pie. The main menu is similarly extensive and features home made pies, curries, lasagne and vegetarian dishes as well as steaks and fish dishes.

The garden to the front overlooks the Downside village green and dogs are welcome. There is a large attractive separate restaurant.

Children are only allowed in the restaurant when dining and in the stable bar.

The pub is open from 11am-2.30pm and 6-11pm Monday to Saturday, Sunday 12-3pm and 6-10.30pm. Food is served from 12-2pm and 6.30-10pm. The restaurant is closed Sunday evening and all day Monday.

Telephone: 01932 862105.

The pub is situated in a private road off Downside Road opposite Downside Common.

Approx. distance of walk: 5 miles. Start at OS Map Ref. TQ 109582.

There is a large car park behind the pub.

The walk commences across the green at Downside, goes northwards towards Cobham past the entrance to Cobham Park, crosses the River Mole water meadows (if flooded use Plough Lane). There is a visit to the Semaphore Tower on Chatley Heath and the return is through Hatchford Wood and across farmland, which may be muddy in places.

1 Turn left out of the pub and cross the green keeping to the left hand edge and turn left past the pond onto a road. Continue to the end passing the entrance to Cobham Park and turn right at the 'T' junction. Just past Plough Lane turn left over a stile by a finger post. Follow the path across the fields past a line of oaks and across a stile and footbridge into another field. Look out for snipe and woodcock here and follow the riverbank round to the next stile. The height of the ancient oaks belies their girth because they have been pollarded over centuries. Cross a footbridge and two more stiles to reach a

stile and gate on to Pointers Road where you turn right.
2 Pass the redundant gateway and lodge to Hatchford Park, now severed from the house by the M25. Reach a Chatley Heath Semaphore Tower signboard, turn left over the M25 and then uphill on a tarmac road. At a fork go right to the Semaphore Tower, one of a chain of signalling stations set up by the Admiralty in the 1820's. If open it is well worth visiting the exhibition and climbing the 60 foot tower. Leave the tower and retrace your steps to the fork where you turn right down hill through sweet chest-

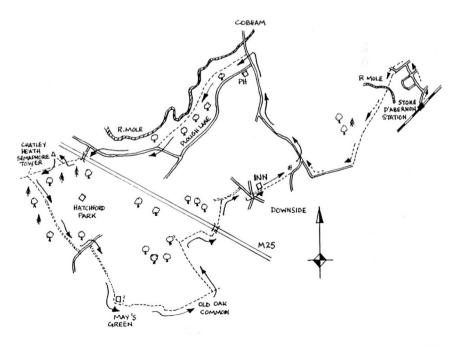

31

Walk No. 9

nuts and rhododendrons. At a three fingered post turn left towards Ockham Lane. Turn left on the lane and just past 'Flowers Cottage' go up steps on the right by a fingerpost. Go through a kissing gate and ahead on an enclosed path and then a farm road with fine views. Where the road bends left go straight on past houses and cross a field to a stile. Continue on a path between fences, over a footbridge and then left across a garden to a stile. Turn left down a road. This is Mays Green.

3 At a fork by 'Willow Glen Cottage' keep right and at the gate to 'Yew Tree Cottage' go over a stile and turn left along the hedge. At the end of the hedge go half right to a waymarked post and then on to another at the edge of a wood. Follow the path through the wood, Old Oak Common. Cross a way-marked stile and emerge from the wood to turn left across a field to another stile, where a fingerpost advises you that Ockham Lane is ½ mile. Maintain direction over three more stiles and fields to reach a fingerpost in the middle of a field, where you turn right. Go through a gateway and down the next field to a fence at the bottom. Turn right and then left to cross a bridge over the M25.

4 Reach a farm gate, cross a stile to the left and turn right down a field with the hedge on your right. Cross a stile at the end by Pondtail Farm and turn right down the farm road. You reach Chilbrook Road and turn right. The inn sign is now visible by the side of Downside Road. Cross over and back to the pub.

Restored Chatley Heath
Semaphore Tower

The Bell, East Molesey

The Bell looks as if its medieval architect and builder were both 'meadoholics', hence its other name 'The Crooked House'. Inside and out it reveals its history. The nautical weather vane was salvaged from the first St Mary's Church which burned down. The two bars are called 'Duval's' after highwayman Claud, who made a nuisance of himself throughout North Surrey and 'Runners' after the Bow Street Runners who pursued him. Once a coaching inn with stabling for 28 horses, the pub also doubled as a post office in the 20th century.

After this illustrious past the pub now falls within the Scottish and Newcastle empire and is managed by Michael Whelan. Real ales on offer include Old Speckled Hen, Theakston's Best, Old Peculiar and Greene King IPA. There is a choice of wines and tea and coffee are always available.

The menu has touches of the exotic with such as Moroccan lamb with minted cous cous and chicken, chilli and coriander puffs; but it is also true to its origins with good old English fish and chips in beer batter and steak and Stilton pie.

The garden is well equipped for children, who are welcome in the pub if seated away from the bar.

The pub is open all day every day and lunch is served from 12-3pm.

Dogs are admitted on leads only.

Telephone: 0208 941 0400.

Walk No. 10

The pub is situated in Bell Road, East Molesey and is reached via Walton Road (B369) and St Mary's Road.

Approx. distance of walk: 3½ miles. Start at OS Map Ref. TQ 146678.

There is parking at the pub and in the street. Also beside the Thames at Hurst Park reached by the A3050 and Saddler's Ride – see map. The walk may be started there or from Hampton Court Station. Both points are on the route. If you can make this a day trip Hampton Court is literally just across the bridge, or there is potential for another walk in the Palace grounds.

The real attraction of this walk is the pub, which must be experienced. Otherwise you get to walk beside three rivers and meander through the streets of East Molesey with their uneasy mix of elderly and modern architecture. There may be surprises for bird watchers along the rivers.

1 Turn left out of the pub. Bear right round St Mary's Church and at Walton Road turn right. At the roundabout turn right into Esher Road, cross over and cross the bridge over the River Mole. Turn left into Summer Road and left again into Molember Road, which leads unsurprisingly to the bridge over the River Ember. Turn left over the bridge and take the footpath beside Seymour House. At the A309 turn left past the weirs marking the confluence of the Mole and Ember and pass Hampton Court Station on the right. Cross Creek Road and bear left pass the Streets of London pub into Riverbank.

2 Immediately fork right onto the Thames Path. Pass Molesey Lock and Molesey Boat Club. Look out for cormorants drying their wings on the weir posts and a lone tern that patrols the river from here to Chertsey.

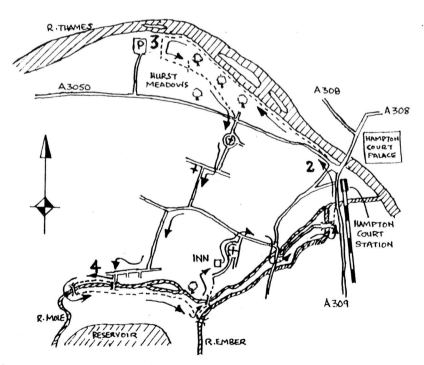

Hurst Park, formerly a race course, is to your left and you reach a 'swan feeding station' by a car park and a Thames Path fingerpost. The swans are outnumbered by Canada geese, gulls and mallard with maybe the odd pink footed goose that has lost its way.

3 Turn left here across the green passing to the right of a basketball court and a children's playground and then turn left on a gravel path. At a 'T' junction turn right and at a Hurst Meadows noticeboard bear right to Graburn Way. The gates to your left were once the gates to the race course. Cross the A3050 into Church Road, bear right round the island site of St Paul's Church and continue down Church Road. Turn right into Vine Road and left into Park Road. At a 'T' junction turn right then left into Seymour Road. Continue forward when the road becomes a track, turn right at the end, then take the third on the left, Green Lane.

4 Before the footbridge turn right on a signed footpath beside the R.Mole. The path goes on for a mile but there is no return route so at the next bridge cross over and turn left down the opposite bank to return. The path leads to a green and you keep to the riverside. Pass a footbridge and cross a road by a weir. Look out for herons here and goldfinches may be feeding on thistles and teasels. Continue by the river to pass a football pitch on the right then turn right across the grass to a gap in the hedge ahead. Emerge on the bank of the R. Ember and turn left. In 150 yds bear left past a gate and cross the R. Mole by footbridge. Go ahead on a path to reach Bell road and turn right back to the pub.

'Feeding Station' on the Thames Path

The Red Lion, Egham

The Red Lion, owned by the Punch Retail Pub Company, has something of a Jekyll and Hyde character. What you see on the outside is a beautifully presented building dated 1521, resplendent with hanging baskets and fascinating details like the square lead drainpipe with carved wooden hopper. Inside it is a typical brash and noisy town centre pub decorated with special offer drinks posters. But The Catherine Wheel had been buried under an office block, it was 2pm and there was no other pub in sight, so it was time to look for the plus points.

The Greene King Abbot and IPA was a definite step in the right direction and there was a good choice of wines by the glass. The patio area to the side was a sunny refuge from the 'music' and the bar staff were welcoming, attentive and thoughtful. One took out a dish of water for a customer's dog without being asked.

The menu was cheap and cheerful – Sunday lunch £5, jackets, fish and chips etc. All in all it was a pleasant experience and the dog owner turned out to be the head gardener on a local Arab potentate's estate, so we learned much about pruning wisteria and managing three wives at once. Only three, not a particularly potent potentate then?

The pub is open all day every day. Food is served from 12-2.30pm and evenings. Children are welcome in the pub up to 7pm and they are certainly dog friendly. Telephone: 01784 432314.

The pub is situated in the car free shopping precinct in Egham Town Centre.

Approx. distance of walk: 4½ miles. Start at OS Map Ref.TQ 010714.

There is parking behind the pub reached via Hummer Road, Crown Street and Runnymede Road. There is a car park (80p for 4 hours) adjacent to Egham railway station and free parking at the recreation ground off the A308. See end of Section 1 of walk and map. The walk may be started at Egham Railway Station. Head down Station Road until you reach a 'T' junction by Barclays Bank and turn right to the pub.

This walk starts beside the Thames, visits three historic monuments, passes through mature oak woods and ends across Runnymede meadows beside a secluded pond.

1 Turn left out of the pub into the shopping precinct and immediately left again into Runnymede Road. This bends right and becomes Crown Street. Continue along here to Hummer Road and turn left. Cross the A30 carefully and cross the meadow on the metalled path following the fingerpost direction Footpath No 12. Cross a road (A308) into Yard Mead, advance to the Thames river bank and turn left. The path leads into a recreation ground in which there is a parking area. Keep beside the river through this most attractive park with weeping willows

along the bank and families of wagtails, mallard, coot and Canada geese.
2 Leave the recreation ground through a gate and continue to hug the river bank for over ½ mile until you see the Magna Carta Memorial in the meadow to the left with a path leading up to it. Cross the road to visit the memorial erected by the American Bar Association in recognition that not only was the constitution of the United Kingdom was based on the principles outlined here in 1215. Leave the memorial and turn left along the path with trees on your left to

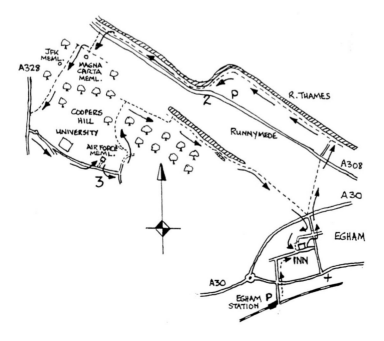

37

reach the entrance to the John F Kennedy memorial, placed on an acre of soil given to the American people following JFK's assassination in 1963. You reach the memorial up cobbled steps and pass it on your right to continue uphill. At the top look right over a wooden gate for a surprise view of Windsor Castle. Keep ahead as the path becomes a track with Brunel University grounds to your left. At a road cross to the pavement and turn left then left again into Coopers Hill Lane. At a 'T' junction go right and at a fork by the University Campus entrance keep left on the main road. Do not pass by the Air Forces Memorial without a visit. Fittingly atop a hill with a constant backdrop of aeroplanes arriving and departing Heathrow, it is a poignant reminder of those who did so much to keep us free in 1939-45. Here are recorded over 20000 names of British, Commonwealth and European airmen who flew with British squadrons and never returned, who have no grave but this memorial. It is a humbling experience. The views from the top of the tower are worth the climb.

3 Turn left out of the memorial grounds. The lane becomes a track and where it bends right turn left on a path by a National Trust Noticeboard. The path goes down hill aided by sets of steps. Ignore all side turnings and keep to this wider stepped path through mature woodland to reach a set of gates before a field. Turn right here on a narrower path and ignore side paths to keep as close as possible to the field edge. Cross a stile on the left, make your way down to Langham Pond and turn right along a faint path beside the pond. Maintain direction over a stile and look out for herons. This path is rarely walked and they are usually there. Go through a kissing gate on the left and cross a footbridge over a narrow inlet to the pond. Continue beside the pond ignoring the longer footbridge. The pond ends and your way is ahead towards houses in the distance. The path may be overgrown but only with grass and you keep ahead to recross the A30 opposite Hummer Road and retrace your steps to the pub.

The Magna Carta memorial

The Lamb, Farnham

There are more pubs in central Farnham than you can shake a Morris dancer at and seven are on the route of the walk. The Lamb enticed us because it is a Shepherd Neame house with three of the Kent brewer's ales on tap – Spitfire, Goldings and Masterbrew. Not all the pubs provide a full menu on Sundays but manager Rob Danson does, with the addition of the choice of three Sunday roasts to supplement the lasagnes, curries, and specials such as breaded plaice in prawn and mushroom sauce.

Rob has also created an award winning roof garden in which, weather permitting, to enjoy the meal. Pots of the chef's fresh herbs are to be found among all the containers of flowers and the stairs keep the staff fit.

The pub has a busy, jolly atmosphere. A purveyor of fresh eggs does a roaring trade at the bar, the staff are welcoming and the locals even talk to strangers.

Children are welcome in the pub but dogs are restricted to the garden during food service.

Lunchtime food is served from 12-2pm, Monday to Saturday and 12-3pm Sunday. Food is also available every evening.

Telephone: 01252 714133.

Walk No. 12

The pub is situated in Abbey Street in central Farnham, a few minutes walk from the railway station. To join the walk from the station follow signs for town centre, cross the A31 and turn right onto the river bank at the bridge – see dotted arrow on the map.

Approx. distance of walk: 5 miles. Start at OS Map Ref. SU 842465.

The pub has no private parking although you may find a space in Abbey Street. Otherwise there are two public car parks en route for which there is a charge and/or a time limit except on Sundays. The nearest is in Lower Church Road. From the A31 follow signs for Town Centre and Wagons Yard. The other is in Hale Road off West Street. Both are shown on the map.

The walk starts beside the River Wey, visits Farnham Park and the castle, traverses farmland with fine views and ends in the historic town centre, where there are many fine buildings to admire.

1 Turn left out of the pub and right at the 'T' junction to cross the bridge over the River Wey and immediately turn right onto the riverbank. Cross a footbridge and then a road and continue on the riverside path. Cross another footbridge-if you brought some bread to feed the ducks there are some sizeable fish here that would relish a share. Turn immediately right and follow the river. At the next junction by a footbridge go left and then right through a car park to rejoin the river. The path bends left away from the river beside a gate and out to a road. At a 'T' junction cross the road and turn left and at the traffic lights cross into St James Avenue. Go forward into Farnham Park past the children's playground and turn left on the grass.

(The path is down in the trees but there is a better view higher up) Continue along the edge of the woods until you reach another larger playground then drop down to the path and leave the park on a lane.
2 At a crossroads turn right and right again into Castle Street past the Nelson Arms. The pavement ends and you go up steps to the castle entrance. This is an English Heritage site and there is an entrance charge. To continue the walk return to the entrance. Turn right back to Castle Street and cross the road to a fingerpost by the drive to 'Bishop's Square'. At a road turn left past 'The Grange' and turn left again at a finger post next to 'Cherry Trees'. At a fork keep left with the hedge on your right

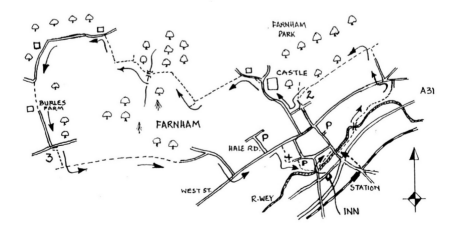

40

and at a crossing path turn right on an enclosed path. Cross a high stile and turn left to another. Go downhill through dense woodland, cross a footbridge and in a few yards fork right uphill. The path enters a field and heads towards trees the other side. Half way to the trees you need to turn right at right angles. According to the state of the crops in the field this path may be hard to find, possibly just a tractor track. Your objective is a gate on the far side of the field. Go through two kissing gates out to a lane and turn left. Stay with the lane as it bears left past 'Lower Old Park'. Cross a bridge and go through a gate on the left by a fingerpost onto an enclosed path. The path becomes a track past Burles Farm and continues to a road.

3 Cross to a fingerpost and up to a stile from which you head straight up to a fingerpost on top of the ridge. Turn left on a path between fields, with fine views all around. At the end of the field go down steps and turn

right over a stile. Cross a stile and a drive and continue on a path. Bear half right across a field and over a footbridge to go up a stepped path. Maintain direction on a drive, cross a road and continue in Wayneflete Lane. This gradually bends left and at a 'T' junction turn right. At the next 'T' junction turn left. Pass Hale Road on the left and at the pedestrian crossing traffic light cross and turn down Church Passage into St Andrew's churchyard. The tomb of William Cobbett, Farnham's most famous son, is by the church door. Leave the churchyard by the east gate under the wrought iron arch and go ahead down the cobbled Lower Church Lane. Turn into the car park on the right and cross diagonally left and out to a riverside path. On the other bank stands The Maltings, formerly the centre of the local brewing trade. Turn right over the road bridge and left into Abbey Street back to the pub.

The tomb of William Cobbett, St Andrew's Churchyard

The King's Head, Frimley Green

Charles I looks a bit whimsical on the King's Head inn sign. That may be because his last journey through Frimley was on his way to have his head separated from his body, courtesy of Oliver Cromwell. The King's Head has been acquired by the Harvester chain so you will know what to expect "as seen on TV". It is not really a pub and, to give them their due, they describe it as "a restaurant and bar", putting the emphasis correctly on the food. The normal range of bar food is available, sandwiches, jacket potatoes, fish and chips, Caesar salad, scampi in a basket, etc. plus children's meals. The restaurant has the standard Harvester menu, and also a choice of dishes offered under the "lunch for under a fiver" umbrella.

There is the usual range of drinks including lagers and frothy 'smooth' beers and Guinness served cold. But no real ale. God knows what Morse would have said. However all is not lost as, weather permitting, you can buy the Guinness and stand it in the sun to thaw out. The food is fine and the staff, all "team members", have been on the course and are uniformly pleasant. I am forced to admit that this a popular venue and most young people will find it all perfectly acceptable, which is why it is in the book.

There is a large garden equipped for children.

Opening hours are 11am-11pm Monday to Saturday and 12-10.30pm Sunday. Food is served from 12-2.30pm daily and from 6.30-10pm evening.

Telephone: 01252 835431.

The pub is situated on the B3012 by the Guildford Road bridge over the Basingstoke Canal, to the south of Frimley Green.

Approx. distance of walk: 5 miles. Start at OS Map Ref. SU 891564.

There is ample parking at the pub.

The walk takes in three easy miles of the Basingstoke Canal towpath, separated by two miles across wooded heathland devoid of all signs and waymarks. There is a good chance of seeing kingfishers along the canal and sparrowhawks in the woods and much else of interest in Frimley Lodge Park and at the Basingstoke Canal Centre. The Canal Centre is one mile from Ash Vale Station via the A321 – see map.

1 Turn left out of the pub and follow the 'South Towpath' sign to the right of the bridge. Pass the miniature railway which is open to the public in the afternoons on the first Sunday of each month from March to October and some Bank Holidays. At the Basingstoke Canal Centre cross the swing bridge and turn right on the other towpath. There is a floating art gallery "Towd Hall", boat trips on 'Merlin' and a canal exhibition open Tuesday to Friday 10.30am to 5pm and weekends from Easter to 30th September from 11am to 5.30pm.

2 Continue out of the centre to a main road and turn left. A few yards past the entrance to 'Potters' on the right turn left on a track. At a gate turn right on a signed bridleway,

the last sign for two miles. It took two hours to find this route with a compass and then find it again to write it down and I was reduced to using anthills as reference points, so you will need to concentrate. Take the right hand fork uphill through woods. Sparrowhawks nest here and you may hear them calling. About 100 yards past the top of the hill, the track begins to bend left, fork right. Ignore two side paths and pass some small wood anthills on the left. The path bends right then left downhill. Maintain direction at a six path junction ie. take the third exit. Pass a couple of wet areas and join another track coming in from the right. Ignore paths to the left and head up the steepish hill ahead. At

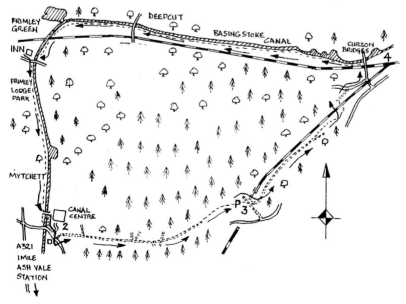

Walk No. 13

the top keep ahead on the main track which goes through a dip then curves right to a car park.

3 Cross the car park to a sign 'No Parking, Emergency Access' by a barrier. Turn right at the sign on a track going towards a road. In 15 yards turn left over a slight bank onto a parallel track and turn right. The railway line is in a tunnel beneath you. The track bends left and there are fine views from the high ground ahead (even better if you climb Longdown Hill to the right). Your path is now down. Keep to the central track past left and right forks then fork left where the main path goes steeply uphill. There are glorious patches of heather but they are receding fast under the onslaught of bracken and birch. No efforts are being made to preserve the heath here as they are on Chobham,

Horsell and Whitmoor Commons. You meet the railway fence and keep with this ignoring side paths. Where the track bends right to a junction take the first narrow path on the left that takes you back to the railway fence. Continue as it widens down to a 'T' junction. Turn left under a railway arch then right. At a road turn right and opposite a tunnel turn left past a barrier.

4 Cross the railway bridge and turn left down the towpath for two miles back to the King's Head. There is much to see on this section. Picturesque locks, banks lined with wild flowers, families of coots and moorhens, dragonflies and damselflies and a real chance of sighting kingfishers. In October there are pockets full of sweet chestnuts and pin sharp images of the trees in autumn colours reflected in the black water.

Swans on the Basingstoke canal

The Cricketers, Horsell

Isolated from any cricket pitch, The Cricketers has in its time been a mortuary, a jail, a work house and a village shop before reaching its present elevated status, what the Total Quality boys would call "continuous improvement". Now it is part of the small Wayfarer chain and owner Bob Morton seems to have hit on a winning formula. The pub is always busy and it is advisable to book for Sunday lunch. There is a wide ranging menu with daily blackboard specials. Pasta is a speciality with several to choose from e.g. lobster varioli, brie and broccoli pasta, penne carbonara and tortelloni. Other popular items are deep fried mozzarella fingers and hot chicken Caesar salad. There is a full range of burgers and a children's menu. The ales always include London Pride or a Fuller's seasonal brew, Old Speckled Hen, Wadsworth 6X and a guest, often the Cornish Doom Bar. There is a good choice of wines.

The interior is atmospheric, featuring old beams and a long bar with a separate dining area one end and a room suitable for families the other end. The large garden is also child friendly with a play area and swings.

Dogs are welcome in the garden but not in the pub.

The pub is open from 11am–3pm and 6-11pm on Mondays to Fridays, Saturday 11am–11pm and Sunday 12-10.30pm. Lunchtime food is served from 12-2.30pm.

Telephone: 01483 762363.

Walk No. 14

The pub is situated in Horsell Birch to the north of Horsell Village.

Approx. distance of walk: 7 miles. Start at OS Map Ref. SU 988595.

There is ample parking at the pub. The walk may be started from Woking Station. Exit next to Platform 1. Cross the road and turn right down Chertsey Road then left into Chobham Road. Head for the town Martian then keep ahead to the by-pass, which you cross via a subway. Exit left from the subway, turn right and right again onto the towpath and pick up the walk in section 3. The subway will be closed until June 2001. Until then cross the by-pass by the traffic lights 100 yards to the left. Cross the wooden footbridge over the canal and turn right on the towpath.

A longer walk for those who really like to work up an appetite, It commences on Horsell Common, crosses farmland and woodland and skirts a lake before taking in a two mile section of the Basingstoke Canal towpath and returning across another part of Horsell Common. You might need a walking stick to tackle nettles on section 1. The walk may be shortened by one mile at the start as follows. (Follow dotted arrows). Turn left out of the pub and join a path and cross a road and continue to cross another and shortly reach a main road. Turn left and in a few yards left again at a barrier into a recreation ground. Follow a fingerpost sign for 'Goldwater Lodge and Lake' and at the next fingerpost follow 'Shops and Health Centre'. Turn left around the lake and then left away from the lake following 'Shops and Health Centre' again to pick up the walk at the end of section 2.

1 Turn right out of the pub, cross a road into Horsell Birch and immediately bear left on a narrow path through a grassy patch. Maintain direction on this path into wood-land ignoring two right forks. At Viggory Lane turn left, cross a road and enter Horsell Common through a set of two wooden gates. Keep ahead over a crossing track,

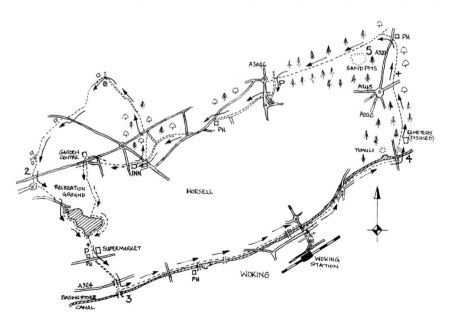

through another pair of wooden gates and along a shady lane. The lane curves left briefly and you enter a nursery. At a 'T' junction go left then right over a bridge. Just past a small pond turn sharp left to pass Deep Pool Farmhouse. Just past the last farm building bear half left to a stile. Go ahead beside a barbed wire fence and then bear left over another stile to continue under trees. Cross a stile, maintain direction across the end of a field and cross a footbridge. Continue on the same line to a metal gate where you enter a grassy path between wooden fences. Just before the end of the path cross a fence on the left by a Footpath sign onto a road. Turn right for a few yards and just past 'Combe Place' turn left over a stile onto a signed footpath. This may be a bit overgrown in summer but soon opens out where you cross a plank bridge and a low barbed wire fence. Proceed down the left hand side of a field to reach a stile in the bottom corner. Maintain direction beside the fence of the next field and cross a stile into a lane. Keep right at the fork and in a few yards opposite 'Tanglewood' turn left. At a 'T' junction go left and immediately right on a narrow path into woods.

2 Reach a road and cross half left to a signed footpath. At a signpost turn left to Goldsworth Park. Enter the Recreation Ground and follow the path to the right signed 'Goldwater Lodge and the Lake'. Reach a road which you cross and turn left. Follow the pavement round to pass the Lodge and reach the lakeside path. Turn right around the lake and turn away from the lake at a signpost for 'Shops and Health Centre'. Continue past Waitrose supermarket, cross a road and maintain direction on a foot/cycle path.

3 Go over a footbridge and turn left on the Basingstoke Canal towpath. Follow the towpath for 1¼ miles. Pass a wooden *footbridge then cross the canal at the next road bridge and join the other towpath. Pass under one road bridge and continue to a second.

4 Go under the bridge and turn up right to · the road and cross the canal. On the far side go half right to enter Horsell Common

through a car park. To your right are the remains of a disused walled cemetery established during the 1914-18 war for Indian Moslem soldiers who lost their lives fighting for the British Empire. At a fork keep left and your path passes between a number of large wood ant hills. At the next fork keep right to join a path coming in from the right. Keep on this path ignoring all left forks to reach a road opposite All Saints Church, Woodham. Cross and re-enter woodland. This section is a good source of sweet chestnuts in season. At the next road by The Bleak House pub cross and join a path next to the telephone box. Continue ahead to meet a wide track where you turn left.

5 After about 200 yards you pass on the left the disused sand pit which was the site of the Martian landing in HG Wells' 'The War of the Worlds'. Keep on this main bridle path to pass through a car park and reach a crossing track in front of wooden posts. Turn left and just before a wooden barrier on the left turn right on a path. At a fork go left and cross a road via the top of the central reservation. Be careful here as it is two way traffic the other side of the reservation. Enter Cheapside and continue to the end. Pass the Plough pub and turn left down the road. Take the first right, Horsell Common Road, and in a few yards turn left on a path. Continue to a lane and where this forks go left back to the pub.

Great crested grebes on
Goldsworth Park Lake

The Hunters Lodge, Knaphill

The Hunters' Lodge, formerly the Nag's Head, dates from 1900 and was acquired by the Bass Vintage Inns Group in 1996. After internal modification it emerged as a most attractive pub with two bars and dining areas on different levels each with log fires in winter. Bass and London Pride are featured with regular guest Hancocks SB and there is an excellent choice of 15 wines by the glass.

The pub is managed with a personal touch by Malcolm and Jo Clark and their menu is extensive in keeping with Vintage Inn standards. Try the "swaddled" Cumberland sausage wrapped in Yorkshire pudding with lambs liver and bacon in onion gravy on a cheddar mash; or, for vegetarians, there is "Rootatouille" - roasted root vegetables in a lentil gravy topped with a baked apple and stilton rosti cake, with a fresh vegetable. Some of the portions aimed at hungry hunters can overwhelm the unwary. The provision of daily newspapers is a nice civilised touch and Malcolm indulges his sense of humour by writing amusing sayings on blackboards. My favourite is "I don't think I will get married again; I will just find a woman who can't stand me and buy her a house".

Children are welcome in the pub away from the bar area up to 9pm and dogs on leads in the large garden only, please.

The pub is open all day 7 days a week with food on sale from 12 noon. There is a large car park to the side.

Telephone: 01483 798101.

The pub is situated on the A322 Guildford to Bagshot road to the south of Knaphill.

Approx. distance of walk: 5½ miles (3½ miles with an optional extension of 2 miles). Start at OS Map Ref. SU 958575.

There is ample parking at the pub. The route passes Brookwood railway station.

The walk starts over the southern edge of Bisley Common, continues across Sheets Heath and ends on an attractive mile long section of the Basingstoke Canal tow path. There is an optional extension through the decaying splendour of Brookwood Cemetery, the largest in Europe. Many of the trees here date from the 1850's when the Necropolis was established as a solution to the gradual exhaustion of graveyard space in central London. There are guided walks on the first Sunday of most months. Telephone 01483 232654 for information.

1 Turn left out of the pub and at traffic lights bear half left on Oak Tree Road. Ignore all side turnings to reach Grindstone Handle Corner (cue for a country and western song?). Just to the left of a Bisley Common noticeboard go ahead on a grassy path. At a crossing path turn right. Pass a wooden barrier, cross a road and continue on the access road to Strawberry Farm. After 120 yards ignore a faint crossing path by a three pronged silver birch and in another 60 yards just past an oak turn left on another faint grass path. (This is to avoid a very muddy bridleway ahead). At a crossing path turn right. Go over the next crossing path to pass houses on your right. Reach a road and turn right and at a right fork keep ahead.
2 Pass the Princess Christian Home and at a fingerpost fork left on Bridleway No. 144. At a fork keep ahead beside the gate and at a fork where the path narrows keep ahead again. At the next fork go left to pass houses. Turn left at a road and fifty yards past a metal barrier fork left on a path beside a telegraph pole. Midway to the next pole fork left on a path into trees. At a fork keep right and at a 'T' junction turn left, negotiate a muddy patch and cross a footbridge. Turn left on a crossing path and left again at the next junction. At a fork bear right to a wooden gate. Go through and straight ahead. Go diagonally across the road to join a footpath and immediately at the fork keep right. Proceed downhill through the gate and out to a road. Turn left and left again before the bridge onto the Basingstoke Canal towpath.
3 Continue on this pleasant stretch for nearly half a mile to reach a bridge. At this point you can opt to continue on the towpath

for another half mile, turn left at a road bridge and back to the pub. Alternatively you can extend the walk through Brookwood Cemetery for another 2 miles as follows. N.B. Dogs are not allowed in the cemetery.
4 Cross over the bridge and keep ahead to Brookwood Railway Station. Go into the station entrance and under the subway into the Cemetery. Turn left on Pine Avenue, then left on Long Ave and right on Railway Ave. Pass a metal barrier and cross a road into the southern section of the Cemetery. Continue on St Cyprian's Ave to the Chapel, now the home of the St Edward Brotherhood

Kingfisher

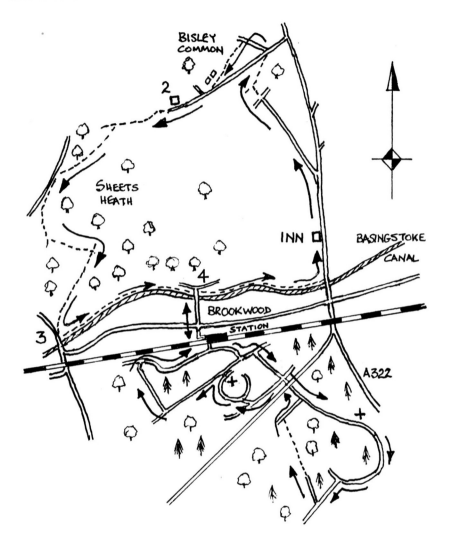

of Russian Orthodox Priests. Turn right here on St. Chad's Ave, which later becomes St George's Ave . Ignore side roads until you reach St. Marks Ave on the left. Turn here and in 130 yards turn right on an unnamed avenue with a parking space in the corner. Pass the memorial to Chelsea Pensioners on your left. The path narrows but keep ahead to a 'T' junction. Turn right and then left to cross back into the northern section. Turn left on Western Avenue and at a fork go right. At a 'T' junction turn left and left

again outside a chapel. Turn left into Long Ave. and admire the magnificent row of Wellingtonia on the left. A gate leads you into the military cemetery, which is far better maintained than the rest. Just past the entrance to the American section turn right. Go through another gate and bear right. The road bends right then left through the Moslem Section and you reach the station entrance. Retrace your steps to the canal towpath and continue where you left off – see para 3.

Ye Olde Windsor Castle, Little Bookham

Now a Chef and Brewer house with the accent as usual on the chef, Ye Olde Windsor Castle dates from the 15th Century when Henry VII's hunting parties roamed the Surrey forests. Descendants of the deer they chased may be seen on the walk. The pub was also a brew house as late as the early 20th century when it opened at 6am to fill the agricultural workers' flagons with ale on their way to the fields.

The décor is warm and comfortable with the old beams, half panelling and inglenook fireplace, complemented by a nice collection of old tables, chairs and stools and flickering lanterns. The pleasant sound track was all lutes and flutes and muted traditional jazz. The tasty snack menu includes shell-on prawns, Italian open sandwiches in ciabatta bread and the house speciality "Hot Hobs" with various fillings. The main menu is on blackboards, Fresh fish dishes are a speciality with novel combinations such as smoked haddock and bubble and squeak. Other offerings include an excellent chicken piri piri, smoked chicken and blue cheese salad, minted lamb loins and several vegetarian dishes, for example, papperdelle pasta and Mediterranean roast vegetables. There is a good wine list including sixteen sold by the glass and ales are Courage Directors and Best and Morlands Old Speckled Hen.

There are extensive gardens and children and docile dogs are welcome.

The pub is open and food is served all day every day from 11am-11pm Monday to Saturday and 12–10.30pm Sundays.

Telephone: 01372 452226.

Walk No. 16

The pub is situated in Little Bookham Street, which can be reached from the A246.

Approx. distance of walk: 5¼ miles. Start at OS Map Ref. TQ 125545.

There is ample parking at the pub. The route passes both Effingham Junction and Bookham railway stations.

A splendid varied walk across farmland, commons and woodland and beside streams and lakes, mostly on firm tracks but with sprinklings of mud through the dense woodland. A birdwatchers delight especially around the lakes and, for those interested in butterflies, Little Bookham Common is a treasure trove, with Purple Emperors present in the oak woods.

1 Turn left out of the pub and after about ¼ mile turn left into Heatherside Close. Bear right and at the end of the road continue on a fenced path. Turn left on a road and in 50 yards left again at a fingerpost into woodland. Go through a pinch stile, cross a small field to another and keep to the right hand edge of the next field. Maintain direction over a waymarked stile and through more woodland. Turn left at a 'T' junction and at the next 'T' junction before a stile turn right on a gravel track. At a gate turn left through a pinch stile. Continue through two more of these (this is definitely not a walk for after lunch) and head diagonally across a field to another where you bear left. There is a path to the lakeside here and a bench to watch the birds from but your route is through the stile by the gate. Then go diagonally right across the field to what may once have been a stile but, in 2000, was a broken wooden barrier. Turn right here with the lake to your right. When the fence ends keep ahead to a stile and then a footbridge. At a crossing track go left then in ten yards right on a path that bridges the end of the lake. Cross the stile and head half left up the field for about 100 yards to turn left over a novel metal stile beside a gate.

2 Go ahead on this residential road to reach

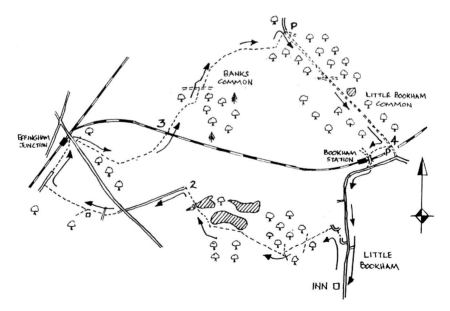

52

a 'T' junction. Turn right and in 35 yards left at a fingerpost. Before 'Squirrels' turn right across grass past a waymarked post. Go through a gate along a garden path and out to a track. Turn right to reach a cricket field. Bear left across the front of the pavilion and continue to cross a stile in a fence. Ignore the path that goes left through a gap and head straight across the common with the trees on your left (there was no discernible path in August 2000). Reach a road at the bottom and turn right past bungalows. The road ends and you continue on a path to reach the Effingham Junction station car park. Turn right at the road and just past a bus shelter on the left turn left into a private road by a waymarked white gate. In 20 yards turn right at a waymarked post. This woodland path may be muddy. Go over a crossing track and a stile by a gate. Continue on a grassy path with a pond to your right. Cross a stile and maintain direction up a field with a small stream and tall bulrushes to your right. Cross a stile, go through a railway subway and cross another stile to join a path between a hedge and a

fence. There may be a surprise in the field to your right – see photo. Cross a stile and a footbridge and enter woodland, another potentially muddy stretch.

3 Turn right on a track and in 20 yards turn left on a path by a Banks Common Sign. Go under a horse barrier and pass a stile on your right and over a footbridge. At a 'T' junction turn left, cross another footbridge and horse barrier. Turn right on a lane for 10 yards then right again. Stay on this track, ignoring side paths, to reach a junction of tracks. Bear half right through short wooden posts past a Merritts Cottage notice board and the cottage and continue on this track ignoring all side turnings for almost half a mile.

4 A few yards before you reach a major junction of tracks and a car park turn sharp right onto a narrow path beside a wooden barrier. Bear left at two forks and continue downhill to a kissing gate giving access to Bookham Station. Cross the footbridge over the line and cross a car park to the road. Turn right, the road bends left and you continue for about a half a mile back to the pub.

The White Hart, New Haw

There has been a pub on this busy bridge and lock site since 1787 when the Wey Navigation was in full swing. A bit square when viewed from the front, the charm lies within and in the garden. In the hands of John and Pat Collins the bar has a good traditional feel with a canal and farming theme to the decoration. There is a smart separate dining area. The ubiquitous Courage Best and Directors is on offer with a regularly changing guest, Brakspear's on our visit. The menu is varied and reasonably priced and there is a daily specials board including soup of the day, main meals such as cajun chicken and a vegetarian dish.

The garden is most attractive bordered by its own tumble pool, the lock by-pass stream, and is well hidden from the busy roads. You can support the wild life by feeding some of your bread to the mallard and sizeable chubb that always appear at lunchtime. There is a slide, swings and a Wendy House for the children but N.B. the stream is unfenced.

Dogs on leads are welcome in the garden but not in the pub.

The pub is open from 11.30am-3pm and 5.30-11pm Monday to Saturday and 12-3pm and 7-10.30pm Sundays. Lunchtime food is served from 12-2pm daily.

Telephone: 01932 842927.

The pub is situated in New Haw Road (A318) on the western side of the New Haw Lock and bridge.

Approx. distance of walk: 4 miles. Start at OS Map Ref. TQ 054632.

Parking at the pub or in a small free parking area the other side of the bridge - see map. The walk may be joined at Weybridge railway station, the start of section 2.

The walk starts at the Wey Navigation, crosses the Wey meadows passing some lakes formed from the river's meanderings and crosses the river. It follows the railway for a mile and then cuts through Weybridge town on paths to reach the bridge that gives Weybridge its name. The return is along the towpath of the Wey Navigation calling in at the picturesque Coxes Lock and Mill.

1 Turn left out of the pub, cross the bridge and after 100 yards turn left on a path at a fingerpost. At a 'T' junction turn left and maintain direction beside a fence and then under power lines. Pass between a lake and a quarry, cross a railway line with care and pass between two lakes. The path bends left and runs parallel to the railway line. Cross a footbridge over the Wey and soon turn right over the railway and left on a residential road. When the road ends go to the left on a footpath signed to Weybridge Station.

2 Pass through a car park with the station on your left. Turn left over the road bridge, then right to join a footpath running beside the railway fence. Bear left away from the railway at a brick wall, turn right through a gateway in the wall and continue on a path to a road. Turn left into a private road and maintain direction at a junction with another road, Windsor Walk. At a 'T' junction turn right and in 50 yards cross the road and turn

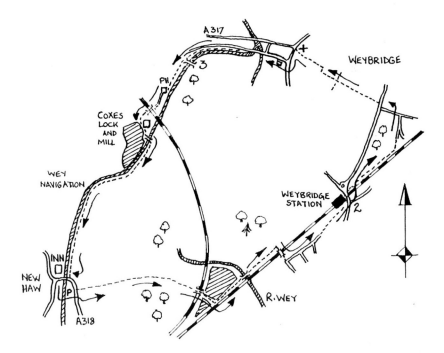

Walk No. 17

left onto a fenced footpath. Pass a playground on the right and the path bends right and left to pass St James' Church. At a roundabout turn sharp left and in 100 yards turn right on Bridge Road past the Queen's Head pub. Cross the bridge over the Wey and the Wey Navigation, then cross the road passing Weybridge Town Lock on your left and join the towpath.

3 At Blackboy Bridge the simple course is to cross the bridge and turn right on the towpath for a mile back to the pub. Or you can go through the gap in the hedge opposite and continue along the right hand bank, through the garden of The Pelican pub and onto the high white footbridge ahead. Cross the railway and continue on a path past the end of a street and the entrance to the mill grounds. Turn left beside the mill pond, cross a footbridge over the mill stream and then cross over the lock and turn right on the towpath back to the pub. Look out for a paddock with Shetland ponies and donkeys on the way.

Coxes Loch and Mill

The Duke of Normandy, Normandy

The Duke of Normandy dates back to 1850 and was acquired by Greene King in 1991. A little bit of history was lost at this time when the inn sign depicting a norman knight in the style of the Bayeux Tapestry was changed. The Duke is a friendly local which has built up a fine reputation based on Val Osborn's home cooking and husband Robin's choice of Abbot and IPA ales. In defence of his lack of guest ales Robin says he prefers to sell two good beers rather than risk guests that may not sell well in competition with the Abbot and deteriorate before the barrel is empty. For a small pub you cannot fault the logic, or the Abbot. But the argument depends on having the two good beers in the first place!

Situated well to the east of the centre of Normandy village the pub has had to work hard to build up a customer base. Now Val's cooking is so famous - Sunday roasts with perfect Yorkshire puddings, fresh fish and chips on Wednesdays, pie night on Fridays, that there is a demand for take-aways. Children are made very welcome with a high slide and a roundabout in the garden but no under 12's or dogs in the pub please.

The pub is open from 11.30am–3pm and 5.30 to 11pm Monday to Saturday and 12-3pm and 6-11pm Sundays. Food is served from 12-2pm lunchtimes.

Telephone: 01483 235157.

Walk No. 18

The pub is situated to the east of Normandy on the A323 Guildford to Aldershot road.

Approx. distance of walk: 4 miles. Start at OS Map Ref. SU 938518.

There is ample parking at the pub. The walk passes within 500 yards of Wanborough Station and may be started from there. Turn right out of the Station into Glaziers Lane. Where it bends sharp right turn left into Flexford Road and follow this when it bends left. Continue to a fingerpost on the left by the drive to the Old Stud Farm. Pick up the walk at point 2.

A pleasant stroll across commons and farmland around Normandy, Flexford and Henley Park, with the chance of seeing deer and varied bird life.

1 Turn right out of the pub and right again into Bailes Lane. Go the end of the lane then forward into woods at a signed bridleway. Ignore side paths, go through a tunnel under the railway and turn right on a bridleway. The chimney on the right is at Flexford Brick Works. Join a lane and continue ahead to a fingerpost on the right pointing up the drive of The Old Stud Farm.

2 Cross a bridge and then turn right over a stile into the garden of 'Little Flexford'. Pass the pool on the right once used as a retting pool to assist in the processing of flax to produce linen. Cross a waymarked stile into a field full of corn marigolds in summer. Bear left across the field to a stile in the bottom left hand corner. Go over a high stile to cross the railway line and enter the field beyond. Keep ahead with the fence on your right and over a stile. Look out for kestrels working the field to your left. The path becomes enclosed and where it enters the next field go behind a rusty gate on your right to keep on the path between fences. Reach a farm road, turn left and in 10 yards right at a fingerless post. Continue along the left hand side of a field. Cross a stile and bear half right towards a barn. Ignore the first stile past the barn and cross the second by a gate. Turn left on a farm drive. At a road turn right and in 40 yards turn left into the drive to 'Newhaven'. The path continues at the end of the drive over two footbridges into a field. Cross a stile and maintain direction up the side of the next long field.

3 At a waymark post, where the field widens to the left, bear half right towards trees. The path is barely discernible you just keep going in a straight line. Pass to the right of the trees through a field entrance, over a track and diagonally uphill across the next field. Aim for a gap in the trees at the top and just before you reach it turn right along the field edge. Cross a stile in the hedge and continue on an enclosed path to reach a house where you turn right. Pass a waymark post on your left, cross a stile and bear half left to China Bridge, so named because the design was copied from a plate. Cross and fork right. Cross a stile and go to the right of two solitary oaks and through a gateway. Continue to a road, cross the stile and turn right back to the pub.

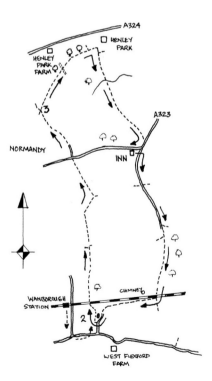

The Black Swan, Ockham

The Black Swan is a big sprawling crossroads free house, reputed to be 400 years old. It is photogenic and has featured in films 'In for Trouble' and 'American Werewolf in London' and episodes of TV series 'Inspector Morse', 'The Bill' and 'The Detectives'. David Williams the licensee for 12 years does his best to make the pub all things to all men. It is wise to enter by the front door where you are met by the heavenly array of 14 real ale pumps. These usually include Tanglefoot, Abbot Ale, Hogs Back TEA, Ringwood's Fortyniner and Old Thumper. In this area walkers and cyclists pore over maps and earnest mouldy fygges, working their way through the ales from left to right, sit quietly discussing traditional jazz and the price of fish. Move to the food counter, with its extensive blackboard menu and home made daily specials and you have to pass the other place, a noisy bar with a dozen lager pumps.

On the day of our visit the pub was hosting a Hell's Angels Convention. The surrounding lanes were full of lurking police cars but it all passed off peacefully without so much as a broken glass. It was a different story 100 years ago when bold lady cyclists pioneering the wearing of trousers were apt to cause ructions in these parts.

There is a large children's playground and dogs are also welcome but, NB, children under 14 are not allowed in the pub, except to visit the lavatories.

The pub is open all day every day and food is served from 12-2.30pm and 6.30-9.30pm Monday to Friday, Saturday 12-9pm and Sunday 12-6pm.

Telephone: 01932 862364.

Walk No. 19

The pub is situated at the crossroads of Old Lane and Ockham Lane at Martyrs Green.

Approx. distance of walk: 6¾ miles. Start at OS Map Ref. TQ 089573.

There is a large car park at the pub.

A walk traversing Ockham and Wisley Commons before passing through the Royal Horticultural Society Gardens and briefly beside the River Wey. The return is across a disused airfield with fine views and over farmland and through woods. Hyde Lane from the airfield is almost always very wet and walking boots are usually necessary. The final section may be a bit of an obstacle course.

1 Turn left out of the pub down Ockham Lane, pass Sendmarsh Tractors and, opposite 'Wisley View' turn left on a bridleway signed to 'Hatchford End'. Hatchford Park is to your right. At a fingerpost follow the bridle path to Ockham Common. Reach a barrier by a fingerpost and go ahead over/under/round the barrier and uphill. Chatley Heath Semaphore Tower is to your right (see also Walk No 9, para 2). At the red waymark post that directs you to the tower bear left, (if you go up to the tower follow the blue car park arrows down again). At a crossing track turn left and follow blue car park direction arrows across Ockham Common to the car park by the A3. Cross the car park keeping to the right of the Café and at a fork keep left parallel to the A3.

2 Cross the footbridge over the road and go between two white posts to a track and turn left. Ignore a right turn and the track narrows and swings right uphill past a house,

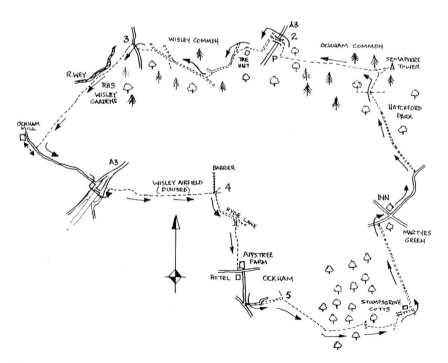

60

'The Hut'. Continue on a narrow path that bends left through bracken and down to a wide sandy track where you turn left. At a fork by a waymark post on the left keep left. In a few yards go over a crossing track. The path narrows and at the next crossing track turn right. Reach a junction of three tracks and take the left fork ahead following the direction of the footpath waymark arrow. Just after the path bends right take the narrower left fork leading into trees and at a crossing path turn left to a road.

3 Turn right then, in 35 yards, turn left to a fingerpost and over a stile onto an enclosed path. The RHS Gardens are on both sides of you for a time and then the River Wey appears on the right. Cross the stile at the end of the path and bear half left across the field opposite. Join an enclosed path and reach a lane. Your way is left but you may wish to make a short detour to the right to see the picturesque buildings around Ockham Mill (see also Walk 23). Retrace your steps down Mill Lane to the A3 approach road. Turn right then left under the arch. On the other side turn left on the pavement, over the bridge and in about 70 yards go up the grassy bank on the right to a stile by a fingerpost. The signed path to the right was impassable in August 2000. Instead go ahead up a wide track onto the runway of the disused Wisley airfield. Keep to the right hand edge of the concrete for a little under half a mile. There are good views all round and a pair of wheatears were a rare sight for Surrey.

4 At a metal barrier across the runway turn right on a narrow path that leads down past a waymark post to a track, Hyde Lane. This is usually very wet even in the summer but you are not on it for long. Turn right over a footbridge and across a meadow, cross a stile and continue down a field with a fence on your left. Cross a stile and join the drive of Appstree Farm. The footpath is to your right but is completely impassable. The owners do not seem to mind the drive being used, although dogs should be kept on leads in case any farm animals are loose. Turn left at the road then right past the Hautboy Hotel. At crossroads turn left into School Lane and where this forks left continue ahead on the drive to School Farm.

5 Go ahead at a fingerpost and in a few yards turn right at the next one. The stile by the gate has been covered with barbed wire so go through the gate and bear half left across a field to double gates, which you will probably have to climb over. Bear half right aiming for a point about 50 yards to the left of the bottom right hand corner of the field. Cross a stile into woods. Emerge on a track and turn right. In thirty yards turn left under a metal horse barrier ignoring any 'private' notices. At a 'T' junction turn left, cross a footbridge and go ahead on a farm drive past Stumpsgrove Cottages. Stay on this drive as it bends left and goes on to the road, where you turn right back to the pub.

Ockham Mill now a private house

The Castle, Ottershaw

The Castle must be a Mrs Mopp's nightmare. The walls and ceilings are covered in collections of brewing and farming implements, horse harness and brasses, saws and weapons including guns, swords, tomahawks and even boxing gloves. This comfortable local originated in the 19th century and proudly proclaims the date of its extension in 1905 on the front wall. The decorations extend to the outside with two ploughs over the door and a patio that has won brewer's awards. Thanks to landlord John Barnard this Vanguard pub has a better ale selection than some free houses, including Abbot, London Pride, Young's Special and Brakspear's bitter.

The staff are particularly welcoming and there always seems to be a knot of "Old Geezers", gaining strength from numbers, chatting up the friendly barmaids. The food is worth coming a long way for and it is not as expensive as some other Surrey pubs providing quality of this class. It all seems to be home made from the soup of the day and the sandwiches to the crab and mushroom flan, fish pie, quiche, chicken curry (with banana), three salads, seven kinds of cheese ploughman's and some mouth watering puddings. This has to be another recommendation for the Good Pub Guide.

Hours are from 11am-2.30pm and 5.30-11pm Monday to Saturday and 12-2.30pm and 7-10.30pm Sundays. Food is served from 12-2pm and 6.30-9.20pm and 7-9pm Sundays. The kitchen is closed Sunday lunchtimes.

Children under 14 are not allowed in the pub and dogs must run the gauntlet of Nelson, the resident Staffordshire bull terrier. He is getting on a bit now but you will know it if he sits on your foot.

Telephone: 01932 872373.

The pub is situated in Brox Road, Ottershaw.

Approx. distance of walk: 4½ miles. Start at OS Map Ref. TQ 022631.

There is ample parking at the pub.

A walk mainly on nursery land and farm land around Ottershaw and Rowtown with the surprise bonus of skylarks singing above the fields around Great Grove Farm and little owls nesting in the woods.

1 Cross the road from the pub into Brox Lane. The road bends left and then right where it becomes unmade. Pass a lake on the left and at a farm entrance turn right then left before the next gate. Pass between fields of herbs and continue along the lane to reach Woodham Park Road where you turn right.

2 Where the road bends right by a Pet Centre take a signed footpath left. At a crossing path turn left and cross the R. Bourne by a footbridge. Continue along an enclosed path between fields, over a drive and eventually to a road where you turn right into Rowtown. Stay on this road for half a mile until it bends up left to a 'T' junction beside the M25.

3 Turn left along Spinney Hill and just past the 40mph signs turn right on signed Footpath No.57. Maintain direction over 3 stiles and at the fourth follow the finger post direction to Guildford Road, Footpath No.56. The next stile and finger post are visible on the brow of a hill ahead. This is a pleasant meadow and in summer you may be lucky enough to hear the soaring skylarks steadfastly making themselves heard above the roar of the motorway. Follow the fence around to cross the stile and head across the field at right angles to the fence. (The finger post for Footpath No.56 had been turned round.) Reach a stile to the left of a metal gate. Cross the end of a small field and another stile, where you bear left round the edge of a field to another stile. Turn left and left again at the next stile still following Footpath No.56. Follow the edge of a blue-bell wood to a stile in the corner. Look out

for little owls here. Go sharp left round bushes and head along the field with the bushes on your left. At a fence turn right and follow this down the field to cross a stile by a gate. Keep ahead to another stile and join an enclosed path.

4 At a road cross and turn left then right down Slade Road. After 100 yards turn left down Spratts Alley. At a 'T' junction turn right, the lane becomes a road and bends right past a school. Turn left into Fletcher Road, pass another school and turn left at a 'T' junction. After 60 yards turn right on a signed footpath. The path narrows then emerges on nursery land. Keep the hedge on your left round right and left bends. At the bottom of the field go over a sleeper bridge to join an enclosed path. Reach Brox Lane where you turn right and retrace your steps past the old thatched cottage back to the pub.

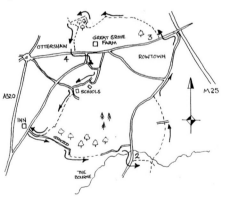

The Royal Oak, Pirbright

The Royal Oak belongs to Whitbread's Wayside Inn chain but this handsome gabled inn has retained its individuality and is to all intents and purposes a superior free house. Manager John Lay organises occasional real ale festivals and issues a quarterly Cask Ale Newsletter. There are never less than six ales on offer and a similar choice of wines by the glass. Not surprisingly the pub features in both the Good Pub Guide and the Good Beer Guide. The interior has plenty of olde worlde charm with log fires in winter. The core of the building was a 17th century cottage and subsequent extensions have been sympathetically done with appropriate materials including old pews and stained glass from a church.

There is an extensive and imaginative menu including wild salmon, smothered chicken, steak and ale pie and a 12oz Aberdeen Angus rib-eye steak. The specials blackboard offers such delights as grilled red snapper, lamb shank, duck breast and pork fillet.

In the summer months there is plenty of room in the large and beautifully kept award winning garden which has a stream down one side. Dogs are welcome in the garden, on a lead please. The pub organises a clay pigeon shoot on the first and third Sunday mornings of each month.

One family dining area is provided but N.B., if this is full children are not allowed elsewhere inside.

Opening hours are Monday to Saturday 11am-11pm and Sunday 12-10.30pm. Food is served from 12-2.30pm and 6.30-9.30pm Monday to Friday, 12-9.30pm Saturday and 12-9pm Sunday.

Telephone: 01483 232466.

The Royal Oak is situated on the A324 Aldershot road south of Pirbright village.

Approx. distance of walk: 4½ miles. Start at OS Map Ref. SU 945543.

There is a large car park to the side of the pub.

The walk is over heathland and through woods on Stanford Common and Pirbright Common also calling in at the tranquil Henley Park Lake. Section 4 may be wet after rain. Take the binoculars for sparrowhawks, little owls and herons on the lake.

1 Turn right out of The Royal Oak and right again at 'Stanford Farm Cottage'. Just past the entrance for Stanford Farm, where the road bends left, turn right on a path at a fingerpost. At a fork go right on a tree lined path through heathland and pass a radio mast enclosure on your left. Look out for sparrowhawks here as there is a regular nest site in the trees to the right. Go over a grassy crossing track and meet a farm track where you go right.

2 Cross a road and continue through a metal kissing gate. Cross a road and go ahead on a wider track. Ignore two paths to the right and keep ahead at a waymark post. At a large grassy area turn right on a narrow path. Aim for the right hand side of the works car park ahead and go beside a barrier to reach a road. Cross at the fingerpost and turn left at a waymark post. Walk parallel to the road for 100 yards then fork right. At a 'T' junction turn right and at a fork

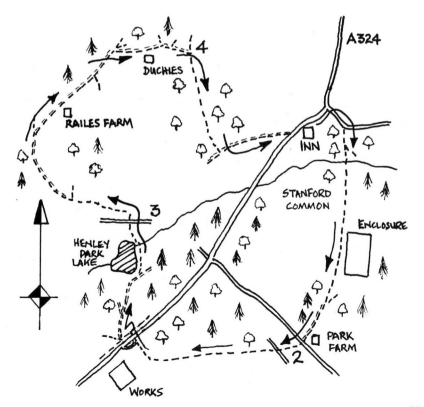

keep left. At a crossing path bear right on the wider path and at a 'T' junction turn left. In fifty yards bear left through rhododendrons and over a footbridge to join the path round the delightful Henley Park Lake. Go in summer for the water lilies and baby waterfowl but avoid Bisley fortnight in July when the incessant firing shatters the peace. Keep to the lakeside (there are views at every fishing station) to cross a footbridge into a car park.

3 Go ahead across a military access road and turn left at a waymark post before a barrier. Go over a crossing path by a MOD notice and turn right on a track with a MOD fence on your left. The track goes uphill and curves right. Pass a stile on your left and just before a sharp rise fork right on a path. Continue past a waymark post by a farm gate. Maintain direction on this main track until at a fork by a gate, with a stile on the right, keep ahead on the right hand track. Pass 'Duchies' and at a crossing track go ahead on the waymarked path.

4 At a waymarked 'T' junction before a gate turn right. Just after a MOD notice board fork right in front of a gate. Go through a tunnel of rhododendrons and emerge with a ditch on your left. There are wet areas here but they are not too difficult to negotiate. Follow the line of the ditch to cross a sleeper bridge and enter a field, which you cross with the fence on your right. Cross a stile into woodland and keep ahead across another wet area and a little humpback bridge and then a stile. Cross a stile by a gate to reach a track by a waymarked post. Turn left, pass Stream Farm Kennels and at the A324 turn left back to the pub.

Henley Park Lake

The Good Intent, Puttenham

The Good Intent was established amid hop fields and oast houses and specialised in locally brewed ales. Now it is that rare thing, a Courage house with a good choice of other ales. As a result it is popular and regularly appears in CAMRA's Good Beer Guide. On our visit featured ales were Greene King Abbot, Young's Special, Theakston's Old Peculiar and Brakspear's Bitter to supplement the Courage Best. Where other pubs have blackboard food menus this one has a blackboard for the ales. This is a small pub with much of the space on one side taken up by a pool table and television. The cosy lounge bar has old beams, pew seats and a winter fire and is frequently full. The small garden also fills up quickly and the locals bring their dogs.

The limited menu specialises in bar snacks, for example, jacket potatoes, omelettes, ploughman's and the more substantial ham egg and chips, seafood platter and vegetarian dishes.

Children are welcome in the pub.

Opening hours Monday to Friday are 11am-2.30pm and 6-11pm, Saturday 11am-11pm, Sunday 12-10.30pm. Food is served from 11.30am-2pm and 12-2pm on Sundays.

Telephone: 01483 810387.

Walk No. 22

The pub is situated in Puttenham's main street, The Street, a few hundred yards south of the A31 Hog's Back route.

Approx. distance of walk: 5 miles. Start at OS Map Ref. SU 932478.

There is a small car park at the pub; alternatively there are large free car parks at The Tarn, roughly the midpoint of the walk, and two on Puttenham Common – see map.

A walk that starts in one of Surrey's last hopfields, climbs to the airy Puttenham Common heathland with fine views and then dives down to a string of ponds in the valley. The return is in woodland up to another high point with the last mile and three quarters over farmland. There is much to interest bird watchers on the ponds and linnets, goldfinches, and yellowhammers in the fields, Section 4 contains a short length of path where a stick to combat the nettles might be useful.

1 Turn right out of the pub and right into School Lane, then left on a track behind the school. Cross a football pitch and walk up the middle of the hop field. Turn left in front of the drying sheds and continue down a lane to a road. Turn left then right into Lascombe Lane. Fork left on Highfield Lane and enjoy the views. Pass a house and in about 150 yards at a fingerpost bear half left across a field to a stile. Continue across

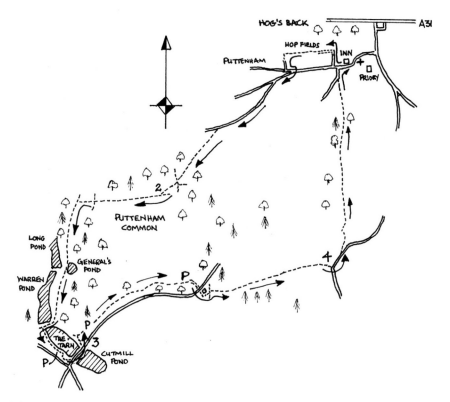

another field and stile to a fenced footpath which leads through a wood. Exit via a kissing gate, turn left for 15 yards, then right on a waymarked bridleway. Go under telegraph wires and across a clearing to turn right on a wide sandy bridleway.˙

2 Stay on this path across Puttenham Common for half a mile ignoring all side tracks. This was the site of the Roman Hillbury hill fort. Reach a 'T' junction before a fence and turn left. The path goes downhill and you pass beside General's Pond on the left. After a short section of boardwalk the path forks and you keep right beside the fence to arrive on the banks of Warren Pond and The Tarn. Take the path to the right between the two, from which there are nice views down both ponds. Follow the bank of The Tarn round to the left and, where it ends at a fishing station, turn right up towards the car park. Just before the car park bear left down to a road and turn left.

3 Just before a small car park on the left opposite Cutmill House, turn left and immediately at a fork keep left. Go up steps to a 'T' junction and turn right on a path. Ignore side paths and reach a large car park. Cross to a fingerpost and take the path behind it, initially running parallel to the road. At a fork keep right on the main path. Pass a post with purple, white and green colour markers and just before the next post fork right. At a

fork before a junction of paths bear right and right again in a few yards at the next fork. Go over a crossing path and bear left at a wider track. At a fork keep left uphill to another large carpark. Cross this and bear right to leave by the access track. Cross a road to a fingerpost to the right of a house and turn left behind the garden. Go down steps to a 'T' junction. Turn left and in 15 yards turn right at a waymark. The path goes beside a fence on the right then across a field with a fence on your left. Go through a gate and over a stile on the right to join a footpath. After two more stiles you reach a road via the gate to Tigden Farm.

4 Turn left and in about 100 yards fork left over a stile by a gate. Bear left beside a hedge and at the end make for a green gate. Just before you reach it turn right on a narrow path up the hill ahead. Continue through a gate on the left and down the field ahead. Pass just to the left of the first oak and aim just to the right of the left hand one of four oaks at the bottom of the field. Cross a stile and bear left to follow a fence up the next field. Cross two stiles to join an enclosed path, which may be overgrown with nettles in season. Emerge over a waymarked stile and continue ahead. Puttenham Priory and Church are visible at 2 o'clock. Cross a stile by a gate and continue on the road back to the pub.

Hop fields Puttenham

The Half Moon, Ripley

Not so long ago Ripley High Street boasted six pubs within a quarter of a mile. The George and The White Horse had been lost but in early 2000 The Anchor met all the requirements of any good pub guide. Just as my pen was poised I was told that it was to be sold to become a Thai restaurant. Alas and alack! Another fine English pub Thaid and died, sacrificed on the altar of lime and coconut milk curry. No matter, the disappointment led me to discover the Half Moon.

A tiny pub with a tinier patio with just one table, this is a welcoming free house nicely decorated with some World War II memorabilia and offering London Pride, Hog's Back Hair of the Hog and a guest, e.g. the Itchen Valley Brewery's Wykeham Glory. Owners Trevor Beale and Paul Trimming have been in charge for 6 years turning this 250 years old pub into a smart little tourist hotel (7 bedrooms), without detracting at all from its cosy pub image on the ground floor. The menu has a good range of pub food including ploughmans and chillies and particularly fine home cooked ham. The house speciality is pizza and they offer a choice of eleven toppings.

Children 10 and over and dogs are welcome in the pub. A younger child bound, gagged and hobbled would probably be admitted to the patio with special pleading.

The pub is open from 11am-2.30pm and 5.30-11pm Monday to Saturday and 12-3pm and 7-10.30pm Sunday. Food is served from 12-2pm and 7-9pm daily.

Telephone: 01483 224380.

The pub is situated on the west side of Ripley High Street (B2215).

Approx. distance of walk: 4½ miles. Start at OS Map Ref. TQ 055569.

There is a free public car park behind the pub, access 100 yards south, and extra parking half way across the village green – see map.

The walk starts across the huge village green of Ripley and goes on to the River Wey Navigation via Ockham Mill. There is abundant interest along the Navigation at Walsham Lock, Newark Lock and Bridge, the ruins of Newark Priory and Papercourt Lock, before branching across farmland beside a 'secret' crop and skirting a lake. Ripley village is a fascinating place with many old buildings and antique shops to explore. N.B. you may need a walking stick to tackle summer brambles in Section 4.

1 Turn right out of the pub and take the first turning on the right beside the car park and across the green. With a car park on your left turn right through a break in the

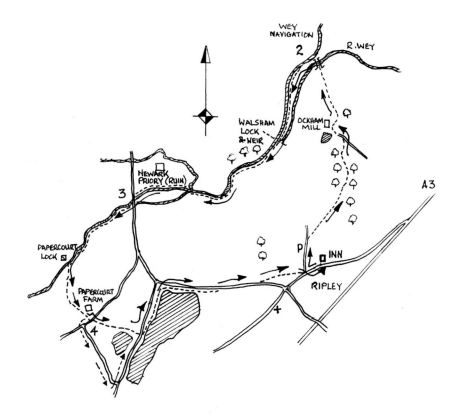

71

low fence before a 'No Horse Riding' notice and fork left across the meadow. Ignore side turnings and enter woods at a waymark post. Follow the bridleway waymarks across two footbridges to a lane. Turn left past 'Millwater' and Ockham Mill, then right at a fingerpost. Pass 'Ockham Court' and cross a stile by a waymarked gate. Continue as the track narrows to a path, cross a footbridge over the River Wey and arrive at the towpath of the Wey Navigation.

2 Turn left on the path between the river and the Navigation to Walsham Lock, where the two separate in a flurry of weir and lock. Cross the weir and continue along the towpath, through a gate, then another. Thirty yards beyond a footbridge, where the Abbey Stream joins the navigation on the right, look right for a fine view of Newark Priory, sacked by order of Henry VIII in 1538. At Newark Lock cross to the other bank and continue to Newark Bridge. On the bridge look left to the site of the old Newark Mill destroyed by fire in 1966. Only the wheel pits remain.

3 Rejoin the towpath with the Navigation on your right. Cross a wooden bridge and go through a metal gate and continue along the bank to a wooden gate. Advance to Papercourt Lock, where the towpath changes sides again but do not cross the footbridge. Your way is left of the footbridge and over a stile by a gate. Follow a farm track over three more stiles the last of which brings you into the yard of Papercourt Farm, which is guarded by some very pretty cats and some Rottweiler geese. Do not turn your back on the latter while stroking the former! Pass the farmhouse and turn right out to the road.

4 At the road turn left for 50 yards then right over a stile at a fingerpost. In August 2000 the field on the left was full of cannabis plants. (For the genetic modification of walkers?) The first 100 yards of this path can get seriously overgrown in summer and if you are the first through for a while a bramble basher will be necessary but perse-

Newark Priory ruin

vere as you are soon on a grassy path between fields. (If it is too bad take the road route – see dotted arrows on map.) Cross a road via two stiles and bear left on a path through a car park and past the Ripley Girl Guide Hut. (Ignore the 'Private' notices.) Follow the path along the side of a lake and round to the right at the end of the lake. At a grassy clearing by a seat go up towards the road on your left and cross a stile into a field. Follow the field edge and at a stile in the fence cross onto the grass verge. Cross a bridge and continue along the pavement to the impressive entrance to Dunsborough Park, where fork left on a path onto Ripley Green. Go ahead past houses on your right and bear right out to the High Street, where you turn left back to the pub.

The New Inn, Send

The New Inn dates from the mid 19th century when it was a pit stop for bargees and others using the Wey Navigation. It benefited from the rebuilding of Cartbridge in 1999, gaining a new frontage and an additional patio area. The expression 'a stiff drink' is said to have originated in the Woking area. Not, as you might imagine, as the accompaniment to a gravedigger's lunch at Brookwood Cemetery but at the New Inn, which doubled as a mortuary at one time. The juxtaposition must have been an irresistible source of black humour. As penultimate resting places go, being laid out on a pub table with a dish of peanuts on your navel and your friends all around toasting your health in the next world has its merits.

The inn also has great appeal for those still living. With a welcoming interior decorated with canal memorabilia, it is popular with locals and with the boating set, who fill the riverside garden in summer.

The food is good, the menu varied, the portions substantial and the service quick. Their speciality is the 'Hungry Platter for Two'. If you finish it you qualify to purchase the T shirt. Landlord Mark Lilley knows his ales and the impressive display of pump clips is testimony to the mouth watering succession of guest ales, on which the Hog's Back Brewery's T.E.A. and seasonal brews are usually featured.

Children and dogs are welcome in the pub and the garden.

The pub is open from 11am-2.30pm and 5.30-11pm Monday to Friday, Saturday 11am-3pm and 5.30-11pm, Sunday 11am-3.30pm and 7-10.30pm. Lunchtime food is served from 12 to half an hour before closing time. Evenings to 9.30pm.

Telephone: 01483 762736.

Walk No. 24

The pub is situated on the south side of Cartbridge, Send, at the junction of Send Road (A247) and Potters Lane.

Approx. distance of walk: 4½ miles. Start at OS Map Ref. TQ 017560.

There is some parking at the pub for both river boats and cars. Otherwise cars can usually be parked in Potters Lane.

On this walk you get two rivers for the price of one, the River Wey and the Wey Navigation canal cut in the 1650's to allow river traffic from the Thames to reach Guildford and Godalming. The route also crosses farmland and gives the opportunity to visit two ancient churches in the villages of Send and Old Woking. There may be mud at the start of Section 2.

1 Leave the pub through the rear garden and turn left on the towpath of the Wey Navigation. Remain on this path for one mile passing Worsfold Gates and Triggs Lock. This is a very attractive stretch through farmland where you should see lapwing and kestrels.

2 About 200 yards beyond Triggs Lock by a footbridge, turn left over a stile and bear half right towards the tower of Send Church. The field may be muddy if cows are in it but slabs of concrete have been judiciously placed to help you across the worse patches. Cross a footbridge over the River Wey at a point where herons frequently fish and turn right on a path. This leads you beside the 17th century Send Court Farm to the gate of the church. St Mary's dates from around 1200 and is in a lovely riverside setting with traditional yew trees, all enhanced by the dovecote on the roof of the old stable block next door. Leave the church and head down the road. There are usually several handsome Spanish Arabian horses in the field to your left. At the end of Church Lane turn right and then left into Vicarage Lane. Pass the Vicarage and turn left at a fingerpost next to 'Cedar House'. Keep on this long straight path for half a mile. Turn right at a road and after 100 yards turn left at a fingerpost beside 'The Larches'. The path narrows and bears left downhill. At a 'T' junction turn right still downhill. The path becomes a lane and at a road cross to Send village green and aim for the right hand side of tennis courts. Cross a road and turn left then right down Wharf Lane. Keep ahead to

the end through white gates and posts along a path to the Wey Navigation.

3 Cross the footbridge. If you wish to curtail the walk you can turn left along the towpath here back to the pub. To continue the walk go ahead on a narrow path, cross a footbridge then a second over the River Wey.

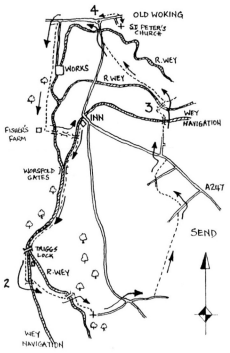

After 10 yards turn left at a fork on a path running parallel to the river. This is Broadmead, the survivor of the three great common fields of Woking. Now it is a haven for birds and butterflies and in summer you should be serenaded by meadow pipits as you pass. The path bends right towards the tower of St Peter's Church, Old Woking. Pass a concrete building to reach a gate to a road and turn right to reach a roundabout. St Peter's Church has an interesting collection of artefacts and a 900 years old oak door depicting a Viking saga about the battle between good and evil. To visit turn right at the roundabout and right into Church Street.

4 To continue the walk turn left at the roundabout. At the drive to the works of the Martin Printing Group turn left over a bridge and immediately fork right over a stile into a field. At a fork go left beside the stream. Do not cross the footbridge but keep ahead to a football pitch. Go down the left hand touch line into woods and cross a stile into a field. Head down the left hand side of the field over three stiles to the drive of Fisher's Farm. Turn left and cross two bridges. Where the drive bends left go forward beside a wall, cross a footbridge and turn left on the towpath back to the pub.

St Mary the Virgin, Send

The Viking Saga door, St Peter's Church, Old Woking

Triggs Lock, River Wey

The Cyder House Inn, Shackleford

The Cyder House Inn used to be a free house with a small integral brewery producing masterpieces such as Piston Broke. Armed with only half the story I withdrew my custom in 1998 on hearing the owner had sold out to a brewery. The half of the story I was missing was that the brewery concerned was the Hall and Woodhouse, Badger Brewery. A very pleasant surprise to be met by a warm welcome and by Tanglefoot, Golden Champion and Badger Best, particularly when the guests were Hog's Back TEA and Gribble's Fursty Ferret. Excellent.

As luck would have it, while enjoying the Thai green curry in the garden, a gust of wind caused my puppodum to become airborne. 'Er outdoors made a great saving catch but in doing so knocked her glass of wine over. Opportunist ingrate that I am I quickly renegotiated the driving duties so that I could sample all the ales. This is definitely one for the Good Pub Guide and the Good Beer Guide.

Phillip and Wendy Nisbet have turned the brewery section into a games/children's room. There is a stylish 'L' shaped bar and smart dining and patio areas in which to enjoy good home cooked food. Offerings include the usual bar food but with imaginative variations such as nachos, ciabatta sandwiches and venison and red wine pie. Vegetarian dishes include avocado and vegetable Stroganoff and vegetable and capsicum lasagne. There are two blackboards to tempt you with starters, main courses and puddings and there is a separate children's menu.

Dogs on leads are welcome in the garden.

Opening hours are Monday to Friday 11am-3pm and 5.30-11pm. Saturday 11am-11pm and Sunday 12-10.30pm. Food is served from 12-2.15pm and 6.30-9.15pm daily.

Telephone: 01483 810360.

The pub is situated in Peper Harow Lane, Shackleford.

Approx. distance of walk: 5½ miles. Start at OS Map Ref. SU 935453.

There is parking at the pub and in the small free car park at the junction with Grenville Road just to the north. The walk passes Godalming railway station. Leave by the down platform turn left and go the end of the car park and turn right down steps to a road. Turn left and join the walk at Point 3.

A walk over farmland and along the Wey Valley to Godalming. There is a hill to start the return then the charming hamlets of Eashing, where the bridges were built by the monks of Waverley Abbey, and Peper Harow.

1 Turn right out of the pub, then sharp right at crossroads into Grenville Road. Turn left into Rokers Lane, which soon narrows to a path with fine views. At a waymark post fork right on the bridleway and at crossroads bear half left across the road past a fingerpost into a field. Keep to the left hand edge and reach the A3 via a kissing gate. Cross the dual carriage way at the break in the central barriers.

2 Go through another kissing gate and straight ahead up the field to a stile by a telegraph pole. Continue across the next field, cross a stile into woodland and bear right steeply down hill on a stepped path. At a waymarked crossing path turn left then right on a track. Pass to the left of 'Milton Wood' and continue on a hillside path with the R.Wey below you. Reach a road and turn right beside the first house, cross a bridge by a pill box and turn left on a waymarked path. At a footbridge on the left turn right on a tarmac path that leads you beside the R. Wey. Continue past a small weir and cross a drive by a gatehouse to reach a road. Turn right under the railway arch, cross the R.Wey and turn right on Vicarage Walk. At a 'T' junction turn right.

3 Pass under the railway arch and head up the road past the Meath Centre. The road goes steadily uphill and swings left past 'Westhangers'. Go ahead at a fingerpost down the drive to 'Shepherd's Cottage'. Leave by the gate at the end and take the

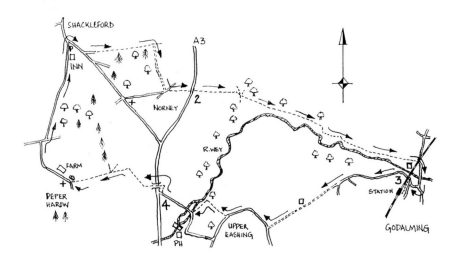

77

right fork ahead, New Way. At a 'T' junction turn right. The road bends left and just before 'Dean Cottage' on the right turn right over a stile. Head straight across the field to a stile and left down steps through woods to the bank of the R Wey. At Eashing Bridges your way is right over the bridges but there are interesting National Trust cottages and the restored Abbey Mill, now offices, ahead, not to mention a pub if you are in need of refreshment. The cottages and 'Tankards' over the bridge have little pieces of ironstone set in the mortar for decoration and supposedly to deter the sparrows from pecking out the mortar.

4 Just before the A3 turn right up a track past a telephone box to cross the road via a footbridge. Go through a gate and turn right on a bridle path. The path bends left and at the end of a field go through a gate on the right. Immediately at a fingerpost turn left through trees, cross a stile and maintain direction up the slope ahead. There are good views to the left. Pass to the left of an octagonal outhouse and reach a road. Turn right pass the small muddy pond which is nevertheless home to some sizeable fish and, on our visit 25 mallard, including 9 day old ducklings hatched in the not very des.res. on the pond. The little church of St Nicholas, Peper Harow, is also worth a visit. In the church yard there is a very old multi stemmed yew that you can walk through. Continue through this pretty hamlet and ignore a fingerpost on the left. Turn right on the road then left on a road signed to Shackleford that leads you back to the pub.

National Trust Cottages, Eashing

The King's Head, Shepperton

The King's Head on this occasion is that of Charles II, believed to have visited this 15th century pub with his mistress. For the same reason it might have been called the Nelson's Arms. The age, if not the stories can be authenticated and this is a bustling atmospheric pub sited opposite the church in Church Square, the original heart of old Shepperton. There is an inglenook fireplace, a separate bar and dining area at the rear, various intriguing nooks and a small courtyard garden.

Owners Deborah and David Longhurst are used to famous faces from nearby Shepperton Studios and can claim an entry in the Egon Ronay Good Pub Guide. Ales on offer are Theakston's Best and Courage Directors. The menu is basic pub grub, jackets, sandwiches, burgers, tortillas, omelettes, and anything with chips and beans for children.

Opening hours are 12-11pm six days and 12-10.30pm Sundays. Food is served to 2.15pm and from 7-9pm but in 2000 the kitchen was closed Friday and Saturday evenings and Sunday lunchtimes.

If you can only do the walk on Sunday there is another pub, Thames Court, en route – see map, section 3.

Dogs are welcome in the pub where a reception committee of two Staffordshire bull terriers awaits.

Telephone 01932 221910.

Walk No. 26

The pub is situated in Church Square, the old village centre of Shepperton.

Approx. distance of walk: 4 miles. Start at OS Map Ref. TQ 077665.

There is very limited parking in the square but ample space in the free car park about 250 yards to the north – see map. The walk passes within ⅓ mile of Shepperton railway station – see map.

This walk starts in an historic village square, crosses the M3 twice meanwhile passing between lakes alive with wildfowl. It concludes along a stretch of the Thames riverbank to Shepperton Lock, with an option to take the ferry to the Weybridge side. Birdwatchers do not forget your binoculars and a walking stick could be useful at the start of the walk in summer.

1 Turn left out of the pub into the square. Cross the road and turn right then left into Cemetery Lane. The path bends right and left down through the cemetery then right between walls. Follow the footpath signs out to a wide path with Halliford Mere to your left and a wild meadow to the right. In summer this is full of tall mallow, teazles, thistles, balsam, golden rod and nettles, a heaven for butterflies and goldfinches.

Ominously this was for sale in 2000. Pass a waymarked post and negotiate a kissing gate to cross a road. There is a footpath ahead well supplied with fingerposts which bird watchers may be prepared to brave for the chance of seeing reed buntings and various warblers. However it can become very overgrown in summer. The easy option here is to turn right along the grass verge to the roundabout then left into High Street and

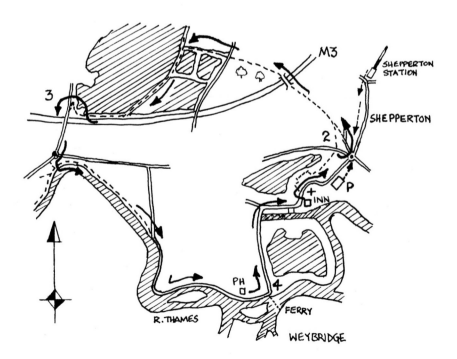

immediately left again into School Lane. (If you parked in the free car park you have the option of going directly to the roundabout – see dotted arrow on map.)

2 Pass in front of the Three Horseshoes pub and at a fork keep left on the path, then left again on the narrower path 'Black Ditch Walk'. Pass a footbridge on your left, the point at which the overgrown path emerges. Keep ahead at the next fingerpost, cross a footbridge over the M3 and maintain direction on a grassy path. Cross a road bearing half left to a fingerpost pointing up a road. The road ends and you cross a stile to a path. At a fork keep right with a lake to your left. At a 'T' junction turn left, now between lakes. At a fork keep left, cross a footbridge and at an immediate fork keep right. At a 'T' junction by a waymarked fence turn right on a path between the lake and the M3. The path ends by bending right then sharp left up to a road.

3 Turn left and cross the bridge over the M3. A wide grass verge takes you down to a roundabout, where briefly turn right into Chertsey Bridge Road then left over a stile onto Footpath No. 40A. Go ahead to the River Thames and turn left along the bank. Pass some interesting houseboats and when the path becomes a road continue on the grassy strip beside the water. The road bends left past Shepperton Lock then left again away from the river at a Thames Path fingerpost. There is a ferry across the river to Weybridge at this point available every quarter hour on request (ring the bell). In 2000 the fares were £1 single and £1.50 return. The service was available during April to September up to 6pm and from October to March up to 5pm.

4 From the ferry station turn left up the road and turn right at a 'T' junction back to the pub.

The Weybridge to Shepperton Thames ferry

The Robin, Sunninghill

Until 1999 the Robin was 'The Old Belvedere', named for Fort Belvedere nearby from which Edward VIII announced his abdication in 1936. Now a hotel with ten bedrooms it was renamed when acquired by the Bass Vintage Inns chain. You will know to expect a spacious comfortable pub with several dining areas, an excellent choice of wines and the Vintage Inns menu, all nicely presented with generous portions. And the ale on offer is Bass and Fuller's London Pride. Music at lunchtime is a matter of personal preference. Pubs with young staff often try to force feed you loud, raucous conversation preventing pop music appropriate to evening sessions in clubs, certainly no aid to quiet enjoyment or digestion at lunchtime. The Robin serves up a delightful mix of standards by Sinatra, Nat King Cole, Peggy Lee, Ella Fitzgerald, Louis Armstrong, Dean Martin and similar vintage played so your ears are just straining to hear them properly. Wishing to complement them on the choice I asked the young bar staff who had chosen the music. In unison, anticipating a complaint, they replied "Sorry about that. It was Head Office not us!" Good old Vintage Inns, leaving nothing to chance, although it left me slightly disturbed that I might share the musical taste of a brewery conglomerate's accountant.

Amid all this programmed uniformity the manager Donal O'Leary, strives to bring some individuality to the scene with his accent on service. He is there on top of the job and there is no shortage of pleasant, attentive smiling staff. An amazing array of sauces and dressings are brought to the table for your delectation and delight and the puddings are "introduced to you" from the trolley. This is a pub where only a churl would fail to leave a tip.

Children are welcome in the dining areas. Dogs on leads in the garden only, please.

The pub is open from 11am-11pm Monday to Saturday and 12-10.30pm Sunday. Food is served from 12-10pm daily.

Telephone: 01344 870931.

The pub is situated on the A329 close to the Blacknest Gate to Windsor Great Park.

Approx. distance of walk: 5 miles. Start at OS Map Ref. SU 980687.

There is ample parking at the pub. The walk may be started from Sunningdale station. Turn left out of the station and walk up the A30 to point 3.

A walk which starts in Berkshire, visits Coworth Park and Sunningdale, enters Surrey and traverses Wentworth Golf Course. The return is through Coworth Park again with a glimpse of Virginia Water Lake. Paths are generally good.

1 Turn right outside the pub and right again on a signed footpath between houses. At a road turn right and enter Windsor Park at the Blacknest Gate. Past the pink painted lodge turn right on a path and at a 'T' junction go right on a wider track. Cross a bridge and continue ahead to reach Blacknest Car Park. Enter through the small gate on your right and cross to the road. Cross over and turn left. At a bridleway fingerpost turn right into Coworth Park. A notice informs you that you are entering Ahmibah Farm. Keep ahead with the polo field on your right. The spire of Sunningdale Church is at 1 o'clock.
2 Pass between two attractive ponds. The 'farm', actually an upmarket housing development, is on the left and opposite here turn right on a waymarked path beside a fence. Stay with the fence past two waymarks, cross a sandy track and go into woods which may be muddy, and out to a road where you turn left. Pass Dale Lodge Road and Coworth Road, an old entry road into the park. At a junction by Trinity Church keep ahead into Bedford Lane. At the end of a row of bungalows turn right on a signed footpath. This path between fields leads you to the A30.
3 Cross the main road and turn left. At a fingerpost to 'Shrubbs Hill Lane' turn right and at a 'T' junction turn right and then left between fences. Go left round a circle of houses and past 'Rosemullion' go left down a path at a signpost. At the end of fences follow the path into woods bearing right behind gardens. At a 'T' junction go left on a wider track and at a fork keep left next to the golf course. Continue on this track through mature pine woods and then as it winds up and left across Wentworth Golf Course. At a fork past a bunker on the right bear right and re-enter pine woods with a fairway on your left. This path curves left across the course to reach a metalled road by 'Silver Birches'. Turn left down this road, 'West Drive', through the Wentworth estate.
4 Reach the A30, cross and turn left. At a fingerpost before a restaurant turn right into a drive. Pass 'South Lodge' and stay on this track as it goes uphill and then down to join a metalled road. You are back in Coworth Park. Pass the 'farm', and retrace your outward path. At the gate turn left back to the Blacknest car park. Cross over and out through the rear gate into Frost Farm Plantation and go ahead towards the lake. Turn left along the lake side, cross a bridge and at a fork bear left to leave the park by Blacknest Gate. Go down the road to a post box on a telegraph pole where you turn left on a footpath and left again back to the Robin.

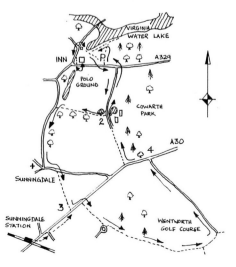

The Wheatsheaf, Virginia Water

The Wheatsheaf, dating from the construction of the Virginia Water Lake in the 18th century and now managed by Chris and Celia Greenslade, is part of the Chef and Brewer chain. It is a smart hotel with 17 bedrooms but the ground floor still has the feel of a large country pub. It is broken up into separate areas and has a bustling atmosphere of bon homie particularly in winter when the fires are lit. There is a conservatory available for private parties and a colourful patio area at the rear.

Diners are catered for on several price levels and with very extensive and appetising menu choices. There is a choice of ploughman's and snacks such as a pint of prawns with marie rose dip; main meals like chicken piri piri, or special restaurant style dishes, e.g. beef fillet stuffed with crab on a pastry crouton in a Madeira sauce. For the last one you are recommended to leave the walking boots in the car and don the Gucci loafers. To complement your meal there is a choice of 16 wines by the glass and 20 malt whiskies. Amazingly, given these choices, the six ale pumps all dispense Courage or Courage. Might this be the pub, I wonder, whose staff made the trip to a local independent brewer and brought back a barrel of alternative real ale for their own Christmas party?

Children are welcome in dining areas, dogs in the garden only.

Opening hours are 11am-10pm every day except Sunday 12-9.30pm. Food is served all day.

Telephone: 01344 842057.

The hotel is situated on the A30 at the eastern end of Virginia Water Lake.

Approx. distance of walk: 4½ miles. Start at OS Map Ref. SU 958687.

There is ample parking at the hotel but NB, entry is via a traffic light off the A30. There is an automatic barrier and a £3.00 charge, that is refundable against a purchase from the bar on production of the parking ticket. There is also a public pay on entry car park next door.

A lakeside walk in Windsor Great Park in beautiful surroundings on good paths with only a few muddy patches in winter months. A good variety of bird life in the woods and on the lake e.g. cormorants and mandarin duck and, in May, a wonderful show of rhododendrons and azaleas in the Valley Gardens.

1 Turn right out of the hotel along the A30 and immediately right on a footpath beside the car park which takes you to the lake side. Turn right and follow the path for ½ mile, where you turn left over the bridge between the lake and Wick Pond. Go ahead to the totem pole presented to Elizabeth II by the people of British Columbia in 1958. From here your objective is the bridge between the lake and Johnson's pond and your route is through Valley Gardens. There is an alternative lakeside path – see dotted arrows on map, but either way you will be tempted to explore the many side paths.

2 From the totem pole go ahead to the sign post and follow the pointer to 'Valley and Heather Garden'. At the next sign post turn left to 'Azalea Valley'. In May as you descend the path the sight and scent of the massed azaleas provide a memorable experience. Bluebells carpet the valley floor. The path is grassed over for a few yards but you continue past two wooden seats, the second of which commands a nice view down to the lake. The path winds down to a road where you turn left and meet the lakeside path.

3 Cross the bridge and veer left on a sandy bridle path and in a few yards go half left again on a grass path towards a large oak tree. At a fork by the tree bear left, cross a drive and pass in front of the Park Wardens' houses. Past 'Flinders Cottage' go half left on a narrow grass path down to the lake and turn right beneath shady beech trees. Reach the road and across the bridge turn sharp left to rejoin the lakeside path.

4 At a T junction turn left over a bridge and left again onto the path along the southern edge of the lake. After one mile you reach a picnic area with some Roman ruins on the right imported from Leptus Magna and erected in 1827 by order of George IV. Towards the end of the lake the path divides. Those with energetic children may wish to take the lower path to the waterfall, otherwise take the higher path. Past the waterfall the metalled path goes up left to the lake but you keep ahead through trees to the hotel car park.

Rose and Olive Branch, Virginia Water

The Rose and Olive Branch has been a pub for about 250 years but I have only just discovered this gem. Originally it was a beer and cider shop on the then edge of Windsor Forest. It is the only pub with the name Rose and Olive Branch. This is supposedly derived from a meeting of Cavalier and Roundhead commanders during the Civil War when a minor treaty was signed and favours exchanged, the rose from the cavalier and the olive branch from the roundhead. As this would have been in the 1640s it must all have occurred in earlier premises but it is a nice story. And it is a nice pub, smart as paint inside and out, small but comfortable and characterful and the original watercolours on the walls are for sale. A Greene King house, their Abbot and Triumph ales are always available together with Ruddles bitter. Kate Dale and Alistair Adam produce a printed menu of usual pub grub and are happy to offer reduced portions of some of these pro rata for children.

The blackboards have to be seen. Seven varieties of pastry Wellingtons, six home made pies including pork in cider and mango, pheasant in sherry and morello cherry and, strictly for the Vicar of Dibley, venison in red wine and chocolate! And home made apple pie to follow. All these at Virginia Water prices of course but still excellent value. This pub must be a contender for the featured section of the Good Pub Guide.

The pub is open lunch times from 11am-3pm and Sundays 12-3pm. Food is served from 12-2.30pm and evenings 5.30-11pm, Sundays 7-10.30pm. I suspect many walkers will want to come back in the evenings.

Children are welcome inside the pub and quiet dogs on leads. There is a pleasant garden to the rear.

Telephone: 01344 843713.

The pub is situated in Callow Hill on the northern side of Virginia Water.

Approx. distance of walk: 4 miles. Start at OS Map Ref. SU 993692.

There is parking at the pub. The walk may be joined from Virginia Water railway station, follow dotted arrows on map. Turn right out of the station into Christchurch road and take the first left, Stroude Road. After half a mile turn right into The Lane and pick up the walk at point 2.

A pleasantly varied walk along country lanes across meadows full of wild flowers and butterflies and through shady woodland with glimpses of interesting buildings along the way. There may be mud in the woods and on bridlepaths.

1 Cross the road from the pub to the pavement and turn left. Where the road bends right cross back and turn left on a bridleway. (The waymark is on the telegraph pole.) At a road turn left and at Gorse Hill House fork right on a path. At a fingerpost follow 'Stroude Road'. The path becomes sunken and you cross a railway line to a lane. Pass a piggery and at a road cross over and turn right.

2 Turn left into The Lane and at the end follow a path that bears left between fields.

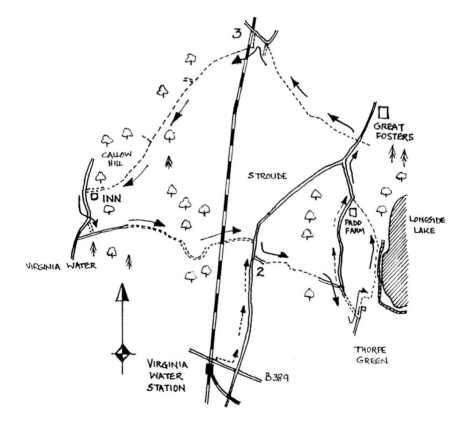

87

Cross a footbridge and continue to a lane where you have a choice. You can turn left along the lane to Padd Farm following dotted arrows on the map. This is recommended in wet weather or high nettle season. Otherwise, turn right and go to the end of the lane emerging by Thorpe Green. Turn sharp left round a fence and through a yard to a waymarked footbridge. Go ahead to a stile and turn right, then a second stile and turn left between a fence and a stream. The path bends left to reach the lane again by the entrance to Padd Farm. Turn right and right again on a main road. Great Fosters is ahead on the right. In about 120 yards turn left on a footpath to Prune Hill. Cross a footbridge and a stile and bear half right across a field. Aim for the arrow post to the left of the right hand house. The buildings on the horizon ahead are the Royal Holloway College. Cross a stile and at a lane turn right, then fork left up Prune Hill.

3 Just before the level crossing turn left on a footpath. Go through a kissing gate and cross the railway to another, then take the right hand path away from the railway. Cross a gravel drive and follow the sign for Footpath No. 42 to Callow Hill. Cross a stile into woodland on a path that rises and falls and may get muddy. Cross a footbridge and join a fenced path with a meadow on the left. In 2000 tree creepers were nesting behind split bark on an oak tree to the left. At a fingerpost keep ahead on Footpath 42 in the shade of fine specimens of oak species, beech and chestnuts and back to the pub.

Bluebell Wood, Virginia Water

The Bull's Head, West Clandon

The Bull's Head is a grade II listed building which has aroused considerable interest including feature articles in the press. It started life as a timber framed hall house dating from c1540. The first mention of the Bull's Head is in 1810 and throughout the 19th century it was owned by the Crooke family who founded the St Nicholas Brewery in Guildford, origin of the Christmas ales no doubt. In the early 1900s' a petition, fortunately successful, against the proposed closure of the pub, describes it as 'a most accommodating house having good stabling and being well conducted, greatly patronised by travellers arriving by train for trips on the Downs and the only place where workmen can be accommodated with lodgings'. It was used by the village football and cricket teams for changing and refreshments and had a slate club with many members. Clearly it was the quintessential village pub and it seems to have retained much of that character today. The stables have been sacrificed for the car park and the pub has been subsumed into the Courage empire.

The pub has been in the same family for 17 years and Diane and Des Locke proudly maintain the family traditions of good home cooking with daily specials and brisk and friendly service. Finding a dining space indoors at weekends in winter can be a problem – as Diane says they are a victim of their own success and tables are not bookable. Real ales always available are Old Speckled Hen and Wadsworth's 6X or a guest, Wychwood's Hobgoblin being most enjoyable at our last visit.

Children and dogs on leads are welcome. The garden is well equipped for children.

Opening hours are 11am-2.30pm and 5.30-11pm Monday to Friday; Saturday 11am-3pm and 6-11pm; Sunday 12-3pm and 7-10.30pm. Lunchtime food is served to 2pm.

Telephone: 01483 222444.

Walk No. 30

The pub is situated on The Street (A247) south of West Clandon village.

Approx. distance of walk: 5 miles. Start at OS Map Ref. TQ 044516.

Parking is to the side of the pub. The walk may be joined from Clandon station. Follow dotted arrows on the map and pick up the walk at point 2.

The walk begins in Clandon Park with a fine house in a setting by Capability Brown, and a visit to an ancient church. The route crosses farmland with memorable views from the high points, passes through old Merrow village and returns across Clandon Park farmland and beside a lake.

1 Turn right out of the pub and right into Clandon Park. Walk up the drive to the house. This is a National Trust property and there is an entrance charge to the house. To continue the walk cross in front of the entrance steps and through a gate where a notice advises you that dogs are not allowed. Turn left through a garden with low box hedging. Before you is a genuine Maori house imported from New Zealand by Lord Onslow. Cross the grass towards it and look back for the best view of Clandon House. Bear right of the Maori house to a path, go through a gate and along an avenue of pollarded trees. At a fork go right up to the church of St Peter and St Paul which originated in the 12th century. If it is open look out for the framed fragment of ancient rood screen depicting the two saints with St Thomas of Canterbury. Leave the church by the lych gate and cross the road diagonally left to a lane between old cottages. This soon reduces to a grassy path beside a field. Listen out for skylarks here. At a road turn left into golf club grounds. Where the road bends left to the clubhouse go through a gateway and turn immediately left on a footpath.

2 Reach a road and cross diagonally to "White Lodge" and take the signed footpath to the right of the drive. Cross a drive and a stile and maintain direction down a grassy path and over another stile. This is a favourite haunt of bullfinches. At a 'T' junction with a farm track go briefly right then left to cross a footbridge over a stream. Go ahead to a fork by a waymarked post where keep right, soon with a field to your right. There are fine views from the hilltop. Maintain direction downhill over a farm

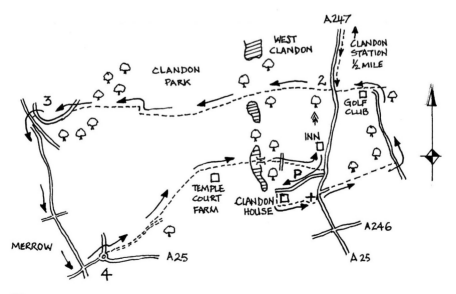

track and along the left hand edge of a field. At the bottom of the field follow the field edge right and then turn left through a gap in the trees and head across the middle of another field. Enter dense woodland and keep ahead to a road and turn left.

3 The road bends right and just before it bends right again go left through a grassy gap, cross a main road and turn left up to Carthouse Cottages. Continue along this pleasant residential road and over a cross roads and past a barrier into Merrow Street. Towards the end there are some fine old properties to admire. Turn left opposite the Horse and Groom pub and walk up to the roundabout.

4 Cross Park Lane and squeeze onto a narrow path to the left of the left hand gatehouse of Clandon Park. This soon leads you onto the narrow drive somewhat out of keeping with the grand gates. Seventy yards beyond the rubbish dump fork left at a fingerpost onto a grassy path through a field. At the bottom of the field bear right through a gap and continue along the right hand edge of the next field to reach a farm track. Your way is straight across and ahead on a narrow, probably overgrown path. Persevere, it is not very long and you reach a waymarked stile from which you can see the route ahead. Continue down to a farm road and cross by way of two stiles. At the second bear sharp left to a stile in the hedge. This leads you onto a narrow lakeside path and over a bridge. Cross a track and continue ahead through trees. Cross a road with Clandon House up to your right, go through a metal gate and turn left back to the pub.

Fragment of Rood Screen, West Chandon Church

91

The Hare & Hounds, West End

The pub is a bit tucked away between West End and Donkey Town but surely deserves to be better known. It is a welcoming Hall and Woodhouse oasis in the North Surrey conglomerate desert. The independent Dorset brewer's Badger beers are permanently available, including the superb Tanglefoot, saintly patron ale of all pub walkers. Also in winter by the warmth of the log fire be sure to try their Robert's Pride named for the brewery's founder. The manager's name is Basil but there is nothing fawlty about his house, he even serves the beer in the correctly badged glasses. This custom, almost universal in Belgium and Germany, is rarely found in England (landlords will say that the nice glasses are too tempting to thieves), but it does add that little final touch to the full appreciation of a glass of the finest ale.

The interior of the pub is spacious with an area for darts and bar billiards on one side of the bar and a dining room on the other. The menu is varied and reasonably priced with children's dishes and home-made daily specials.

There is a large garden with swings and even swinging boats, and a couple of high chairs so children of all ages are clearly welcome. Dogs in the bar on leads only, please.

The pub is open from 12-2.30pm and 5-11pm daily, the kitchen is closed Sunday evenings.

Telephone: 01276 858161.

The pub is situated in Brentmoor Road, West End, a turning off the A322.

Approx. distance of walk: 6½ miles. Start at OS Map Ref. SU 943610.

There is parking in front of the pub and at the roadside.

The walk visits Bronze Age tumuli on Brentmoor Heath, crosses West End Common and Bisley farmland also calling in at a 17th century manor house. This is a figure of eight walk (3½ miles + 3 miles) enabling you to opt to take lunch in the middle or to do half the walk only.

1 From the pub cross the road to a green and follow the fence. At the corner of the fence turn left and go through a barrier. At a fork keep left, ignore paths to the right and at a wooden barrier turn right on an unmade road. Where the road bends left go

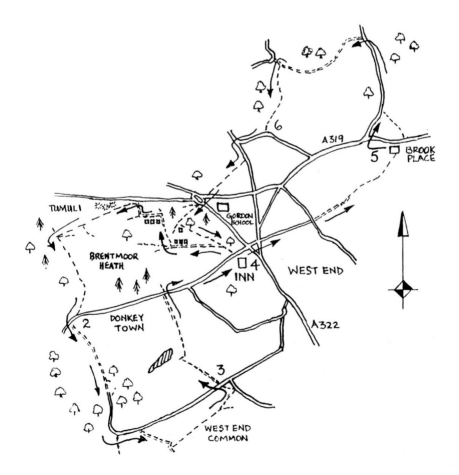

ahead into Brentmoor Heath Nature Reserve and take the left hand one of three paths. Opposite 'Yew Tree Cottage' turn left on a path. At a 'T' junction turn right and by a notice board keep right uphill. There are nice views to the left. At a crossing track keep ahead along Bridleway No.129. Just before a road turn left at a waymark post. At a fork go left. A Surrey Wildlife Trust Noticeboard has information about the burial mounds to the right. It is worth looking out for redstarts, stonechats and Dartford Warblers on this walk. At a fork go right on a wide track and pass a waymark post on your right. Reach a MOD fence where you turn left on a broad track. Pass a metal barrier and turn right at a road opposite 'Heath Cottage'.

2 After about 100 yards, before a MOD noticeboard, turn left on a farm track. Cross a bridge over Trulley Brook and at a fork before barns keep left to reach houses. Follow the road as it bends round to the left and after 150 yards turn right on the drive to 'Heath Lodge', etc. Pass the last house and the path narrows to reach a lane. Turn right and just past a West End Common noticeboard, turn left on a path across the common. At a fork keep left. The path narrows and may be muddy.

3 At a road turn sharp left at a fingerpost onto another footpath. Reach a road and cross to a fingerpost leading up a farm track churned by tractors. Cross a waymark stile by a gate, then another, and head down the left hand side of a meadow to a third. Turn right here, cross a sleeper bridge and bear half left across a field to another stile. Maintain direction across another field and a concrete bridge to a stile by a gate. Follow this path out to Brentmoor Road and turn right back to the pub.

4 From the Hare and Hounds turn right up the road and cross the A322 into Streets Heath. Cross a road and continue beside Streets Heath walking along the green to the left. Pass between tennis courts and a small pond, which was restored recently as a village project. Turn right at a road, Streets Heath again, and then left down Fairfield Lane, which becomes a waymarked path. Cross a stile and keep ahead on a farm track through Pankhurst Farm. Cross a concrete track by a barn and go ahead on a narrow

waymarked path. In a few yards by a waymark fork right. At the next waymark go over a crossing path into a field with a fence on your left and keep ahead to join a drive. Pass greenhouses on the left and turn right through a gate and left along the drive of Brook Place out to the road. Brook Place is a nicely maintained 17th century manor house with shaped gables now run by a Christian charity as a retreat.

5 The footpath from here to Halebourne Lane (see map) has been blocked off due to a dispute between the landowner and the local council over responsibility for the safety of a foot bridge. Until it is resolved the alternative route is to turn left up the road and then right into Halebourne Lane for nearly half a mile, where unfortunately there is no pavement. Pass 'Pandemonium' and at a fingerpost turn left onto Bridleway No 41. Follow this shady path until you reach a footpath fingerpost by a redundant stile. Turn left here, cross a footbridge and at a waymark post turn left. Cross a waymark footbridge, then another and turn right over a third and a stile into a field. Go round the right hand side of the field to a stile. Cross this field to another stile in a fence and then go half left to a stile a little to the right of the field corner. Cross onto a track and turn left through a five bar gate by the entrance to Hookstone Farm.

6 Turn right down the lane and at a 'T' junction go left for 100 yards then right at a fingerpost onto Footpath No 130. Follow the direction of fingerposts through woods and diagonally across two rugby pitches in the Gordon School playing fields. At the far side another fingerpost directs you down a track but where this bends left in a few yards you go ahead on a path to reach a roundabout. Cross the road on your left to the Gordon School sign, then turn right to cross the Guildford Road. Turn right on the pavement then left under a barrier into woodland. Go ahead on the bridleway and where paths cross it just before a fork turn left on the second path, directly opposite the waymarked post. Pass a house down on your right and go downhill to a fork where you bear left and continue to a wooden barrier. Go through onto a green and at the corner of a fence turn right to the pub.

The Barley Mow, West Horsley

The Barley Mow is a Grade II listed building dating from the late 16th century and the oak beamed interior is authentic. During repair work a priest hole was discovered still containing a piece of mouldy bread and a hazel cudgel, later kept behind the bar to deter the unruly. For thirty years the pub was in the hands of the Woodiwiss family. When Mrs Woodiwiss retired in February 2000, the story is that local businessmen got together to purchase it to preserve its individuality from the attentions of the conglomerate wrecking crews. The result is that, under new manager Tim Norman, the pub has lost none of its friendly local character, although it has lost Mrs W's wonderful collection of pig ornaments that decorated the bar. The real ale policy remains the same with a choice between London Pride and Adnam and Brakspear bitters and Greene King IPA.

The lunchtime food is varied and reasonably priced, including such as avocado and Brie salad, home cured ham, egg and chips and various jackets including curry of the day. Tuesday is fresh fish and chip night, served from 7pm, and an enticement to make this an afternoon walk and just hang around afterwards. There is a separate dining area and a two room bar plus an attractive garden.

The pub is open all day every day and lunch is served from 12-2.30pm.

Children and dogs on leads are welcome in the bar and, as the photograph shows, horses are served at the door. This one turns up at 11am every Monday for a carrot.

Telephone: 01483 282693.

Walk No. 32

The pub is situated at the north end of The Street, the main road through West Horsley.

Approx. distance of walk: 4¾ miles. Start at OS Map Ref. TQ 079536.

There is ample parking fore and aft of the pub. The walk may be started from Horsley station – see map.

The walk begins on farmland across the estate of West Horsley Place and continues through Sheepleas, mature woodland virtually flattened in the hurricane of 1987 and now regenerating. There is a visit to the ancient West Horsley Church with its fascinating interior and the return is across fields of golden corn, (or bare earth, green shoots or stubble according to season, so late July is best).

1 Turn left out of the pub and pass some interesting old property either side of the railway arch. Turn right into East Lane and right again into Lollesworth Lane. Cross a railway bridge and turn left briefly and then right on a waymarked path with a field to the left. The path beside the railway line is the one from Horsley station and you can join the walk here. Enter woodland and maintain direction on a signed bridleway to the left of a gate. Lollesworth Wood to your right is in the grounds of West Horsley Place. Stay on this path down the middle of a large field and at the bottom of the field keep ahead on a tree lined track. The track bends right to West Horsley Place Farm where you take the signed footpath to the left of a barn to meet a drive where you turn left. The building with the clock tower was the stable block in the 17th century. Reach the A246 and turn left along the pavement. 2 Just after the West Horsley sign board on the right cross the road and enter woodland by a bridleway signpost. Keep on this wide tree lined path to Sheepleas. Pass a charcoal burners kiln on the left and the path curves right. At the second of two adjacent crossing tracks go left at a waymark post. The path goes steadily uphill. Cross a grassy crossing path and at a junction of paths take the left fork in front of you. Pass a seat on the left and ignore a right fork. At another junction of paths by a waymark post maintain direction uphill and at the next junction turn right at a waymark, now with a field on your left. Continue downhill through extensive new deciduous tree planting. A path comes in from the right and you go over two crossing paths in quick succession. Your path is dotted with yew trees and there is a mature

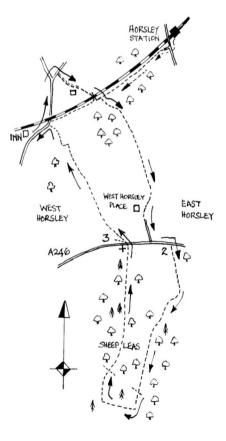

St Mary's Church, West Horsley

beech copse down to the left. Hawfinches can often be seen in this area and woodpeckers and nuthatches abound. At a fork go left down to a path through the beech woods that survived the 1987 hurricane and turn right. Stay on this wide path ignoring crossing paths. Pass an entry to a field on the left and at a fork go left between a beech and a yew on a narrower path. At a 'T' junction go left on a wider path again, now with a field over to the left. At a fork keep left, go through a gap in a fence and keep ahead through a car park. Leave by the exit signs to arrive at West Horsley Church, which hopefully you will find open. It has a number of interesting features the most notable of which is the 13th century wall painting of St Christopher, patron saint of pub walkers and other travellers. This was discovered under layers of plaster in 1972.

3 Cross the road from the church with care as visibility is limited to the right, and go over a stile by a fingerpost. At an immediate fork go forward to a wire fence. Turn left along the fence and keep it on your right. Continue when it becomes a hedge. Maintain direction through two large fields and at the end go through a gap and turn left following the waymark. The path follows the field edge and then bends right towards a railway bridge. Halfway up the field cross

a stile on your left and follow the waymark to a second stile and out to a road which you cross and turn left back to the pub.

13th Century wall painting of St Christopher

The Old Crown, Weybridge

The first recorded licence at the Old Crown is dated 1729. More recently this free house has been in the same family for over 40 years and the current owners are Mark and Yvonne Redknap. A central bar serves the lounge, saloon and snug and there is a conservatory extension to the lounge bar and a patio garden outside. A further separate riverside garden is beside the car park. Surprisingly for a free house the only ales on offer were Courage Directors and Best with Brakspear's bitter 'coming'.

The menu is well balanced offering basic pub grub, sandwiches, burgers, jackets and omelettes. More substantial fare includes three fresh fish and three vegetarian dishes daily and more from the Specials Board, for example, asparagus quiche and beef and horseradish casserole. It is all nicely presented and the pub is busy and popular.

Children are welcome in the lounge bar, conservatory and garden areas but not in the saloon and public bars. There are no apparent restrictions on dogs.

Opening hours are 10.30am-11pm six days and 12-10.30pm Sundays. Food is served 12-2pm and from 7pm. The kitchen is closed Sunday and Monday evenings.

Telephone: 01932 842844.

The pub is situated in Thames Street, Weybridge, near the junction with Walton Lane.

Approx. distance of walk: 4½ miles. Start at OS Map Ref.TQ 076656.

There is some parking at the pub and in the free public car park on the corner – see map.

This is a figure of eight walk giving you the option to take lunch in the middle. The first half is along the Thames towpath and around Desborough Island. The second half picks its way across channels at the confluence of the Thames and the Wey, takes in a stretch of the Wey towpath as far as Weybridge and returns along a residential road and footpaths.

1 Turn left out of the pub. At the corner go through the public car park to the Thames towpath and turn right. After 100 yards there is a ferry to Shepperton. Details of the service can be found in walk 26, para 3. Pass under a road bridge and at the second road bridge turn up steps to cross the bridge to Desborough Island.

2 Where the road bends left keep ahead on a lane at a finger post. Later, where the lane bends left keep ahead on a footpath between the river and playing fields. At a fork with a field on the left keep ahead. Just before a Surrey County Council Open Space notice go briefly left then right on a grassy path. The path bends left rejoining the river bank. At a fork by an iron girder standing upright go left on the gravel path up to a road. Cross the bridge over the river, turn right down

steps to the towpath and retrace your steps to the pub.

3 Turn down the path between the pub and the public toilets. Cross a road and continue down Church Walk. Just past number 16 turn right and over a footbridge. At a road bear half left to the footpath. Cross the footbridge over the River Wey at Thames Lock and turn left down the towpath. Cross a footbridge over a weir. Pass under a road bridge and at the second bridge turn up right over the footbridge.

4 Turn left across the road bridge and then left into Portmore Park Road. Negotiate a roundabout to continue along this residential road. After ½ mile turn left down Radnor Road. Where the road bends left keep ahead on a footpath back to Church Walk and retrace your steps to the pub.

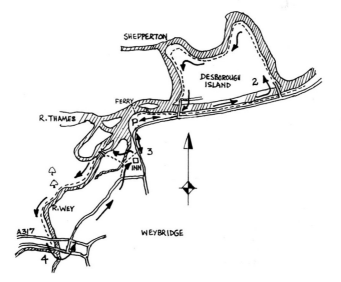

99

The Half Moon, Windlesham

The Half Moon calls itself a "Traditional Free House" and is a perfect example of a traditional 'proper' pub. Not being beholden to a brewery to determine their priorities, owners Helga Sturt and son Conrad can decide for themselves where to spend their money and what choice to offer their customers. One place that money is spent is on the lovely garden, winner of the Surrey Heath in Bloom Competition. This also contains a children's play area including a boot house. Not surprisingly the pub features in the Good Beer Guide. But the House of Commons Beer and Food Award? So this is where they sneak off to for beer for questions? The hardest task here is selecting the ale from the dazzling choice, which will probably include Ringwood's Old Thumper and Forty Niner, Hop Back Summer Lightning, Hog's Back TEA, Triple FFF Moondance, Theakston's Old Peculiar and more. Also popular is Old Rosie cider and there is a good range of wines.

The menu is extensive and there is a separate section of children's meals. 'T' bone steaks and fresh cod and chips are available and a variety of appetising salads. There is a choice of fourteen sandwich fillings on white or wholemeal bread, toasted if you prefer, a dozen different fillings for jacket potatoes, steak and kidney pudding and three egg omelettes. Coffee in variety and tea are always available. The prices are Windlesham but still represent good value for money given the quality of the food, the presentation, the ambience and the service.

Children and dogs are not allowed in the bar area.

Opening hours are 11am-3pm and 5.30-11pm Monday to Saturday and 12-3pm and 6-10.30pm Sunday. Food is served from 12-2.15pm and 6.30-9.30pm. The kitchen is closed Sunday evenings.

Telephone: 01276 473329.

The pub is situated in Church Road, Windlesham Village.

Approx. distance of walk: 4¼ miles. Start at OS Map Ref. SU 928638.

There is ample parking at the pub.

This walk circles the village of Windlesham on bridle paths and quiet roads and visits an attractive arboretum containing several lakes, where herons abound.

1 Turn right out of the pub past the church. Just past Rectory Lane turn right across a field at a finger post. At the next finger post go right to reach a lane. At a 'T' junction turn left and maintain direction via a kissing gate along a farm track heading for the clamour of the M3. Go to the right of a metal gate and keep ahead to cross the footbridge over the motorway.

2 Turn right on a signed bridleway running parallel to the M3. You are now in Windlesham Arboretum. Keep ahead at a bridleway fingerpost with a lake on your left, cross a footbridge and turn left at a way-marked post. Turn left to cross another footbridge and then right on a footpath between a lake and a stream. This delightful section is enhanced by water lilies in season. At a crossing track follow the waymark arrow left but pause to admire the vista down the next lake. Turn right at the bridleway fingerpost and emerge at the side of the lake with a lovely view ahead. Maintain direction through a five bar gate, past houses and out through the main gates to a drive.

3 Ignore a fingerpost on the left, pass a car park and at a road turn left then right down Hook Mill Lane. After nearly half a mile pass a nursery then turn left on a signed bridleway Scutley Lane. This leads to another footbridge over the M3 and on to a road where you turn left. At Pine Grove turn right and opposite 'Homeland' go left on a signed footpath through woodland, across a footbridge and down to a road opposite The Sun pub.

4 Turn right then left up School Lane. At a recreation ground turn left and take the right hand path with the playground to your left. At the end of this bridle path turn right into Kennel Lane then right again to Hatton Hill. Pass a day nursery and turn left onto the footpath and drive to 'Wych Elms'. At a road cross half left and continue along the footpath. Turn right at a drive then left through the churchyard. The mediaeval church was burned down following a lightning strike in 1676. It has been rebuilt twice and was being extended in the summer of 2000. Turn right out of the churchyard back to the Half Moon.

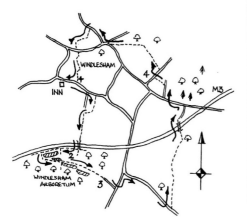

Heron

The Bleak House, Woking

The Bleak House was named for Dickens' novel with the same title. In the late 19th and early 20th centuries it may well have occupied a bleak site perched on the edge of Horsell Common, a mile outside Woking opposite the small settlement of Anthonys. The M25 changed all that and suddenly it was on the main road in and out of Woking and well placed to pick up the passing trade. The common to the west of the pub is probably the most popular dog walk in the area so the pub is always busy.

Manager Sean Ashenden is also the chef and the menu has an international flavour including Mexican and vegetarian dishes and stir fries. The home battered cod is always popular as is the Californian salad. There is a daily specials board above the bar. Ales on offer are Tetley's, Bass and Burton's. The pub is cosy with gas fires in winter.

Children and dogs are welcome inside and the garden at the rear adjoins woodland.

The pub is open from 11am-3pm Monday to Saturday and 12-3pm Sunday, with food served to 2pm and evenings from 5pm.

Telephone: 01483 760717.

The pub is situated on the A320 Chertsey Road one mile north west of Woking.

Approx. distance of walk: 4½ miles. Start at OS Map Ref. TQ 016610.

There is ample parking at the pub.

A pleasant woodland walk mainly on bridle paths, which may be muddy in winter, finishing across Horsell Common with a chance of sighting Dartford warblers.

1 Cross the road from the pub, turn right then left into Anthonys, an unmade road. At a fork keep left and left again at the next fork. Where the track bends left by a house go ahead on a signed footpath. The path has been diverted to skirt the McLaren motor racing premises. Follow the perimeter fence as it curves round a newly constructed lake. At the end of the fence cross a footbridge over the Bourne and go ahead into woodland. Emerge to cross the end of Fairoaks airfield. Pass the windsock and continue on a wooded path to reach an unmade road and then a main road.

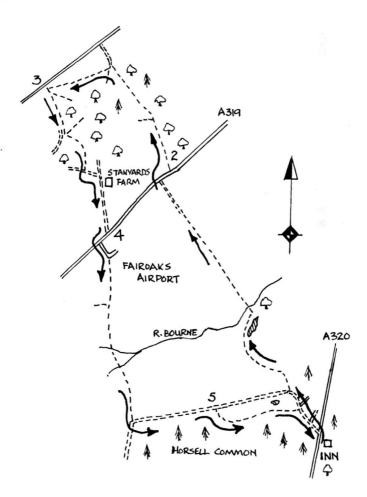

Walk No. 35

2 Turn right and after 100 yards turn left into woodland on a signed bridleway. Maintain direction past two Bridleway Link signs. Stay on this path ignoring side paths as it curves left and then descends to a wooden barrier before an unmade road. Turn left before the barrier on a signed bridle path. Continue on this path with houses to your right to reach a junction of paths at Gracious Pond Road.

3 Turn sharp left back into woodland signed 'Bridleway Link to Youngstroat Lane'. In a few yards at a fork go right. At an unmade road round new property bear left and at an immediate fork keep left on the wider path. At a fork by a Bridleway Link sign go right down hill. Reach a lane and turn left past Stanners Hill and at a fork go right past 'Stanyards Farm'. This was once the home of Sir Edward Banks who built the Waterloo, Southwark and London bridges. There is a piece of the old Waterloo Bridge mounted on a block in the garden. Continue down the lane to a road where you turn right then left into Fairoaks Airport Western Entrance.

4 Keep ahead past Blocks C1 and C2 and where the road bends left go ahead on a signed footpath. Pass the end of the runway, cross two footbridges and continue ahead. Just before a house the path goes left then right and widens temporarily. Continue ahead to the corner of a lane where you turn left. Pass two driveways on the left to reach a green metal barrier by a wire fence enclosure on the right. The lane will take you back to Anthonys and the pub but you may prefer to try the more attractive route across Horsell Common as follows :

5 Turn right at the barrier, go over a crossing path and at a fork go left on the narrower path across heathland. Go over two crossing paths and at a wider crossing path turn left into pine woods. Pass two wooden barriers and your path bends up to the right. At a crossing path go left and immediately keep ahead over a crossing path. At the next crossing path turn right. Stay with this wider track as it crosses heathland and look out for Dartford warblers (nesting in gorse on the left in June 2000). The path enters pine woods and at a crossing track with houses visible to the left turn left to reach Anthonys, where you turn right and right again back to the Bleak House.

"Chip off the old block"
Piece of the old Waterloo Bridge at Stanyards Farm

The Royal Oak, Wood Street

Following the earlier book I was taken to task by the local branch of CAMRA for "walking past one of the finest pubs in Surrey". The awards to substantiate their claim for the Royal Oak are displayed on the walls of the bar. The emphasis is on the real ales and in February 2000, landlord Tony Oliver produced his one thousandth guest ale, the specially brewed 'Oliver's Tipple', courtesy of the Hop Back Brewery. Nice timing for the millennium year. Hog's Back T.E.A. is a permanent fixture and there are always four guest ales including one mild.

Tony and his two sidekicks, Jim and the 'other' Tony, are all gentlemen of a certain age with old-fashioned standards of service. They make you welcome, offer you a taster if you can't make up your mind which ale to choose and even present you with a list of fresh vegetables of the day, so that you can customise your main meal. Superb value. Somewhere in the back is Mrs Tony, a chef of no mean ability – try the Mexican chicken. Many brewery policy makers and pub managers would benefit from a visit here to learn about giving the customer choice, value for money and relaxed friendly service.

The garden is equipped for children with a windmill and swings. Children are welcome in the pub if dining and dogs outside food service times.

Lunchtime food is served from 12-2pm but N.B. the kitchen is closed on Sundays. If you can only do the walk on that day there is another pub on the route, The Cricketers, - see map.

Telephone: 01483 235137.

Walk No. 36

The pub is situated in the centre of Wood Street Village.

Approx. distance of walk: 5½ miles. Start at OS Map ref. SU 958510.

Parking at the pub is limited but can be found in side streets nearby.

This is a varied walk making a wide circuit around the village of Wood Street across farmland and common land where nightingales still sing and through woodland. You may encounter mud and nettles in season.

1 Turn left out of the pub along the main road and turn left down Pound Lane. Pass a wooden barrier, cross a railway track and pass Wildfields Farm on your left. At a fork go left along the edge of a field to a telegraph pole where you turn left to reach the drive to Wildfields Farm. Turn right then left over the railway bridge. At 'Woodside Cottage' follow the direction of a bridleway signpost across grass and two drives to enter woodland. Keep right at two forks and maintain direction to cross the drive to Chapelhouse

Farm. Cross grassland to a waymarked post. Guildford Cathedral is now visible over to the right. Keep ahead at the waymark and in 50 yards fork left downhill. Go over a crossing path and the path curves gently left down to a telegraph pole and on to a road where you cross by a Broadstreet Common noticeboard.

2 Turn right, ignore a footpath sign and about 15 yards after crossing a stream go left on an unsigned path. Pass houses on your right, go over a footbridge and reach a

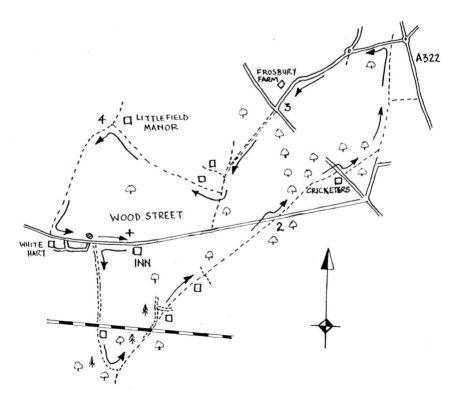

road by The Cricketers pub. Cross the road and turn right then left on a path next to the inn sign. Go uphill through woods to a clearing and continue to a road. Turn left and where the road bends left by a postbox keep right on an unmade road. Keep ahead where the road becomes a path. At a road turn sharp left on a path and then right on a road by a Chitty's Common noticeboard. Keep ahead where the road becomes a path. At a fork go right, join an unmade road and at a road turn left and left again at a mini roundabout. The road curves left past farm entrances and the Grade 1 listed Frosbury Farmhouse with lilyponds in the garden.

3 At a 'T' junction cross to an unmade lane and go ahead to pass 'Hook Farm' on your right. At a waymarked post by the drive to 'Dunmore Farm' maintain direction on the right hand narrow path. Just past a white painted house before the path enters woodland fork right across the grass and cross a sleeper bridge to a path by a fence. Cross a drive and a waymarked stile. Continue over more stiles and a sleeper bridge. You may encounter mud before the next stile. This leads to a wider track which curves right towards the now visible 'Littlefield Manor'.

4 Twenty yards before the track enters the Manor grounds turn left over a wooden footbridge and left on a path across a clearing, through woods and then beside a barbed wire fence. The fence ends and you go up left then immediately right on a grassy path. The path winds through woodland and then enters a field over a waymarked stile. Following the direction of the arrow set sight on a point mid way between two telegraph poles at the bottom of the field. Cross a stile and sleeper bridge and follow a path beside a fence to a road where you cross and turn left. Walk down the side of Wood Street village green past the maypole and village pond, home to some sizeable carp, and continue along the road back to the Royal Oak.

The last Maypole in Surrey, Wood Street village green

The White Hart, Wood Street

The White Hart dates from the 17th Century when it was a cottage with an associated blacksmith's shop and later wheelwrights. The garden wall is a reminder of these origins with examples of the modern blacksmith's art depicting various village scenes. It first became a beer shop in the 1850's and at one time there was a skittle alley.

In 2000 a new management team of Michael and Anita Phipps took over and have maintained the emphasis on real ales, with at least four on offer, usually including Gibb's Mew's Bishop's Tipple, Old Speckled Hen, Old Peculiar and guests. There is also a good selection of wines and malt whiskies. The interior is authentic olde worlde with oak beams and a through fireplace adding cheer to both sides of the large bar area in winter.

There are separate lunchtime and evening blackboards offering a wide selection of good value meals. Specialities include a 16oz 'T' bone steak, fresh whole sea bass and stuffed duck breast. There is a separate dining area and it is advisable to book for Sunday lunch.

Children and dogs are welcome inside and in the garden.

The pub is open all day every day except Saturday when they close between 3 and 5.30pm. Food is served from 12-2.30 lunchtimes.

Telephone: 01483 235939.

The pub is situated in White Hart Lane at the western end of Wood Street village green.

Approx distance of walk 5½ miles. Start at OS Map Ref. SU 953510.

There is parking at the pub. The walk passes within 500 yards of Wanborough Railway Station and the walk may be started from there. Turn right out of the station and left into Flexford Road. Fifteen yards before the junction with West Flexford Lane turn right through an arch in the hedge and pick up the walk at point 2.

A favourite walk with considerable historical interest through an area of abundant wildlife. It commences across Backside Common, a protected "unimproved pasture" where nightingales may still be heard. There is a visit to the Great Barn and tiny 13th century church of Wanborough, once owned by the Cistercian monks of Waverley Abbey. The walk crosses the Hog's Back with fine views in all directions, briefly joins the North Downs Way and returns across farmland and through woods. There is one steep climb on the return over the Hog's Back and a few muddy patches.

1 Turn right out of the pub down White Hart Lane and continue when the lane becomes a path. At a waymark post fork left before a sports field and continue down the left hand edge of the field and then on a path beneath telephone cables. At a fork bear right to join a parallel path and go under a railway arch. Turn right and at a fork keep right. You are in nightingale country but you will probably only hear wrens, blackcaps and whitethroats. Pass a waymark post and at the next post (devoid of direction arrows), where the path turns left, go ahead into a field. The path has been obliterated. It should bear half left down to a gateway onto West Flexford Lane but the tractor tracks suggest that the farmer wants you to go straight ahead to the bottom of this long field, then turn left and right to reach the lane. Anything to oblige. Turn right along the lane and continue to the junction with Flexford Road on the right.

2 In 15 yards turn left through an archway in a hedge into a garden. Cross a stile and head down the garden with a stream on your right. Cross a stile and at the bottom of the field cross the stream by means of stepping stones and then a stile into a field, Go directly across the field to a (gateless) gateway in the hedge and then follow the left hand edge of the next long field. Look/listen for kestrels, partridge, skylarks and yellow hammers here. Cross a stile and maintain direction past a pond, once a fish farm for the monks, to a road where you turn left.

The entrance to Wanborough Barns and St Bartholomew's church is signed about 150 yards on the left. In the church look out for the memorial to members of the Special Operations Executive, SOE, who died in the 1939-45 war. The manor house was their training headquarters. From the entrance to the churchyard fork right between hedges on a bridleway. Go steadily uphill between the residences of foxes, badgers and rabbits. The hedges restrict the views but there are enough gaps to get the idea of rolling fields of barley on all sides or a lot of chalk and flints according to season. Cross the dual carriageway A31 via the link road. At the other side turn right for 30 yards then left to cross a waymarked stile. Enjoy the view then follow the left-hand edge of the fields over two stiles. Cross the drive to Greyfriars Farm and another stile. Go diagonally across the field aiming 20 yards left of a shed to cross a stile and maintain direction onto a golf course with a tee to your right. This is a groundsmen's dump but plough through it or round it to a waymarked gateway. If that has gone on the bonfire too just carry on down hill in a straight line to pass a golf green on your right then through bracken to a waymarked post. Cross a fairway with the 11th tee on your left. Your way is now clear through three sets of white posts and down to a path between gardens.

3 Emerge on the drive to Monks Grove Farm and turn left on the North Downs Way. At a fork keep left past houses and at a junc-

Walk No. 37

tion of tracks turn left on a signed bridleway. Go over a crossing track and, where the track enters a field, fork right on a grass path. Pass a house on the right and continue steeply uphill to the A31. Cross via the link as before and cross the waymarked stile by the bus stop. Head directly across the field over two stiles and into trees. Cross a drive and turn left on the next drive to pass 'Flexford Cottage'. Later pass Flexford Farmhouse and at a crossing track by a house keep ahead towards Bushey Farm.

4 Go round the nice new gate and past the farmhouse, derelict in 2000. Continue on a narrow path through a long tunnel of bush-

es where there may be mud. Emerge at a waymark post and turn right through the railway tunnel then turn right again on the bridleway. The path follows the railway then bends left and you reach a footbridge comprised of four railway sleepers set in the path. Turn round and pace back 25 yards and turn right. (Due to other paths being blocked this link has been virtually obliterated hence the convoluted directions.) Make your way through grass to a faint path going right. It becomes plainer as you go on to reach a fence and turn left. Continue as the path becomes a road back to Wood Street Green and the pub.

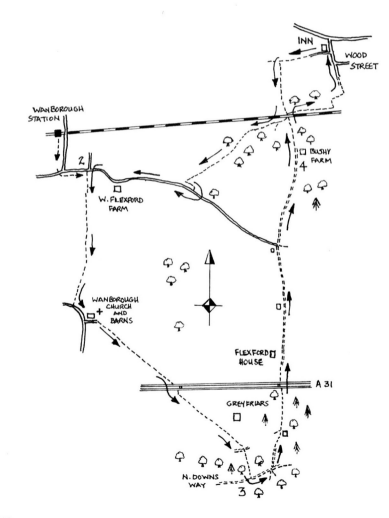

The Fox, Worplesdon

Alan and Christine Watkin took over this rather mangy Fox in April 2000 and set about restoring it to a bright and friendly local, concentrating on appealing to families with a well equipped play area in a large garden. A novelty is a listed outside lavatory complete with cat flap (home to Mr Mistoffelees and Old Deuteronomy?), which they plan to convert into a children's toilet and baby changing area.

Adults are catered for inside with Shepherd Neame's 'Spitfire' on offer as guest ale in this Courage house and similar promised to follow. There are two bars, one with a dart board and the other with a dining area.

Food is served from 12-2pm daily. The menu is extensive ranging from sandwiches up to daily blackboard specials e.g. Mississippi chicken and chicken in garlic marinade and Sunday roasts all reasonably priced.

Dogs are welcome.

The pub is open from 12-3pm and 5-11pm Monday to Friday, 12-11pm Saturday and 12-10.30pm Sunday. Food is served from 12-2pm daily.

Telephone: 01483 236984.

Walk No. 38

The pub is situated north of Worplesdon just off the A322 in Guildford Road. Traditionally the address has always been known as The Fox at Fox Corner.

Approx. distance of walk: 4 miles. Start at OS Map Ref. SU 963548.

Parking is in front of the pub.

Starting in Worplesdon the walk traverses Pirbright Common and nursery land to Pirbright village and a historic church with African connections. The return is another route across Pirbright Common with a chance of sighting unusual birds and animals.

1 Turn left out of the pub and left into Heath Mill Lane. Pass the mill and about twenty yards past the bridge fork right into woodland. Go over a crossing path and at a fork keep ahead on the main path. At a junction of paths keep ahead again. Turn left on a road and immediately right down a drive

signed 'Springbok' and 'The Glebe'. The drive ends in gravel and you go ahead on an enclosed path and through a kissing gate to a road where you turn right.

2 After about 80 yards turn right down the drive to the picturesque White's Farm House. Just past the house at a fingerpost

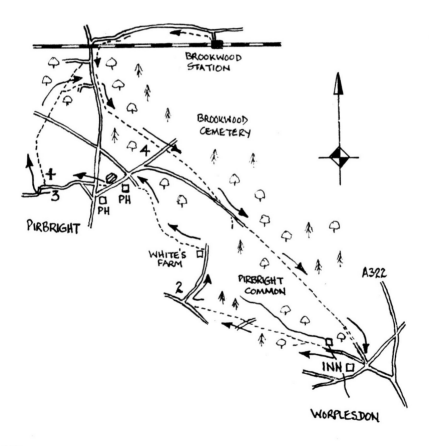

turn left behind the garden border and over a stile into a field. Bear half left to a waymarked stile on the edge of woodland. Cross a footpath and follow the waymarked path through the woods to nursery grounds. Maintain direction through the nursery to a waymarked crossing track and turn left to go out the nursery gate. At a road turn left past The Cricketers pub and the village pond then bear half right across the end of the green, over a road and past the bus shelter to a road junction by 'The Old House'. Turn left towards the church of St Michael and All Angels. Enter the churchyard by the gate and turn down the path. In front of you is the huge granite memorial stone to Henry Morton Stanley, the explorer who 'presumed' to meet Dr Livingstone at Lake Tanganyika in 1871. The church was rebuilt in 1783 to replace an earlier church destroyed by fire. It exhibits one feature common to churches further south in Surrey – little chips of ironstone set into the mortar supposedly to deter sparrows from pecking it out.

3 Leave the church by the lych gate and turn right at a fingerpost along the side of the church. Cross a road and continue on the footpath. At the corner of a fence turn right across a road and pass a playground on your left. Cross another road and keep ahead to a main road. Cross and enter woods and immediately turn right on a path. The path bears left to cross a drive and continues in woods.

4 Go between two houses and cross a road at a fingerpost. The path is waymarked over three sleeper bridges and then across a road to continue on a bridleway. Reach a residential road and turn left. Continue ahead where the road becomes a track and opposite 'Wyndrush' bear left to a Pirbright Common noticeboard. Take the left hand tree lined path. Nightjars nested close to this path in 2000 and the male flew down the path, perched then circled round and landed on the path behind us. A magic moment for a bird watcher. At a crossing path keep ahead

and at a fork keep right on the wider path. At the next fork keep ahead. The track widens uphill then down and leads into Malthouse Lane. The first house has some huge sheep in the field at the back. Before shearing they look like yaks and they don't 'baa' they 'moo'. I kid you not. At the end of the lane turn right back to the Fox.

Grave of Henry Morton Stanley

The Jolly Farmer, Worplesdon

The Jolly Farmer started life as an isolated beer house in the late 18th century. Present owners, Woking architect Anthony Fielding and his wife Savine, acquired the property in 1997 and have fully restored it using new materials. This provides a rare opportunity to see something of what the old oak framed buildings that are now so much admired must have looked like when they were new. It also demonstrates that there are some fine craftsmen still operating in the Woking area. There is a bar with two dining areas suitable for groups and a separate dining room attractive enough for any special occasion dinner. Outside is a landscaped garden and a terrace with tables under a pergola. There is a good wine list and ales regularly featured include London Pride, Abbot, Hogs Back TEA, Timothy Taylor's The Landlord and usually a guest.

Fish and meat are fresh daily and the blackboard menu offers a mouth watering selection. But be warned that as the food is all fresh there are limited portions and early birds get the best choice. As you might expect prices are a little high but still represent excellent value. Sunday lunch is very popular and booking is advisable.

Children are welcome. Dogs on a lead in the garden only, please.

Opening hours are 11.30am-3pm and 6-11pm Monday to Saturday and 12-3pm and 6-10.30pm Sunday. Food is served from 12-2pm and 7-9.15pm. The kitchen is closed Sunday and Monday evenings.

Telephone: 01483 234658.

The pub is situated in Burdenshott Road off the A320, Woking to Guildford road.

Approx. distance of walk: 5 miles. Start at OS Map Ref.SU 987543.

There is parking at the pub and in a public car park next door and also in Salt Box Road – see map. The pub is approximately one mile from Worplesdon railway station. Follow the dotted arrows on the map.

The walk crosses Whitmoor Common, an area of Special Scientific Interest, SSI, comprising bog and dry heath, visits St Mary the Virgin church, Worplesdon and passes cottages once used by Huguenot settlers who set up a local blanket manufacturing industry. The return is via the Merrist Wood College and their tree nursery, Rickford Common, Goose Rye, where orchids bloom, and Brook Pond.

1 Leave the pub through the rear garden, turn left across the car park and a drive to a green. Bear left to a Horse Ride fingerpost and join a path that runs beside the railway line. After about half a mile, at a fork before houses, bear right across a clearing and go between waymark posts into woods. There are two paths running parallel to the fence on the left. Keep on the wider right hand one. Go over a crossing path just past a three colour waymark post with a road visible up the path to the left. Cross a car park and follow the Horse Ride path. At a junction of paths in a clearing maintain direction taking

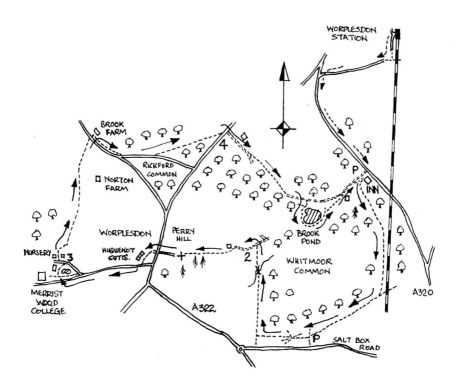

115

the third exit, a sandy path going down a slight slope. Reach a crossing path 30 yards from a road on the left and turn right. Cross a footbridge and continue beside a fence.

2 At a 'T' junction by a waymark post turn left on a track. Keep ahead when the track forks right to a house and in 10 yards fork left on a narrow path that runs beside a fence to a stile. Bear half left across a field passing to the left of a lone plane tree to reach a stile in the corner of the field. Join a dark path oppressed by leylandii, which leads into the churchyard of St Mary the Virgin, Worplesdon. Pass to the right of the church and out the lych gate. Continue ahead to cross the A322 to the drive opposite and turn left on a path at the back of the green. The cottages to your right were occupied by Huguenot settlers fleeing from religious persecution in France in the late 17th and 18th centuries. Pass the cottages and turn right on a lane. Go to the left of two gates to join the drive to Merrist Wood Agricultural College. At a junction maintain direction on a gravel path. Pass a pond (mind the crocodile) and turn right before a building.

3 Turn left at a road and right through a waymarked pinch stile into Nursery grounds. Go ahead and at a fingerpost bear half right on a nursery track. At a fork keep ahead, cross a stile and keep to the right hand side of the field. Negotiate a novel 'lift-up'stile and maintain direction over another field and reach the A322 again via two stiles and a footbridge. Cross the road to the gate to Brook Farm and turn right on a grass path beside the road. Turn left into Goose Rye Road and left at a fingerpost opposite a Rickford Common noticeboard. This path may be churned by horses and muddy. Cross three drives and at a road turn left then right at a fingerpost onto a private road to 'Gooserye' and other houses.

4 In about 100 yards just beyond the sign for 'Pond House' is a triangular patch of wild orchids that bloom in June and July. At a fork by 'Gosling Cottage' go left on a driveway. Pass the gateway on your left and go ahead on a path beside gardens. Cross a drive and continue on a wide grass path. This narrows and runs under telegraph wires. Turn left on a road and just past a speed hump turn right on a narrow path to a footbridge. Turn right over the bridge, follow the path as it bends left under telegraph wires, then turn left on a faint path which soon runs beside Brook Pond. There is almost always at least one heron fishing here so a quiet approach may bring dividends. The path bends away from the pond to a fence. Bear left through the gap at the end of the fence. Pass a seat and at a fork keep right to reach a lane. Turn right and right again beside a gate to cross a green back to the pub.

Huguenot cottages, Worplesdon Green

The Sandrock, Wrecclesham

The Sandrock won the local CAMRA branch 'Surrey Pub of the Millennium Year' award and was second in the all-Surrey competition, so it seemed a natural choice for this book. On arrival it was immediately clear that the award to landlord, Andy Bayliss, was not for exterior decoration or gardening. Inside, however, is a smart, welcoming little free house. There is a public bar with pool table and TV on one side and a saloon bar with a collection of pump clips on the beams and an ever changing array of eight real ales. Holden's Black Country Best and Cheriton Village Elder were served in perfect condition. Andy could give lessons in the cellarman's craft to many bar staff in trendy pubs raised exclusively on lager, who somehow contrive to turn a good ale into freezing pond water.

Andy also does the cooking with the same attention to detail in selection of suppliers and fresh ingredients. Specialities include the 'legendary' club sandwich and burgers to the 'kaighins' recipe. You are invited to select your own topping for the fresh cooked jacket potatoes and the ploughmen's choices include a fresh paté, e.g., chicken liver with white wine and pepper. The specials board usually includes steaks and one or more vegetarian dishes. Overall the pricing represents excellent value for such quality fare.

Well behaved children and dogs welcome.

The pub is open all day from 11am-11pm and 12-10.30pm Sunday. Hot food is served Monday to Saturday lunchtimes only from 12-2.30pm, although evening parties can be catered for by appointment. If you can only do the walk on Sunday lunchtime, the Cherry Tree in Rowledge does Sunday lunches and is on the route of the walk – see map.

Telephone: 01252 715865.

Walk No. 40

The pub is situated in Sandrock Hill Road, Wrecclesham, which can be reached from the A31 and A325.

Approx. distance of walk: 6½ miles. Start at OS Map Ref. SU 830444.

There is limited parking at the pub other than at the roadside. One solution would be to park in the public car park next to the Forest Inn car park (shared entrance) off the A325, (SU 816439), which is on the route and start the walk from there – see map.

The walk starts and ends in Surrey on the lanes of Wrecclesham and Rowledge and passes converted oast houses, reminders of the brewing traditions of the Farnham area. Crossing into Hampshire there is a pleasant stroll across the Wey meadows and a contrasting march on Forestry Commission tracks through Alice Holt Forest. One short section can be very wet after rain.

1 Turn immediately left out of the pub down the track at the side. Cross a footbridge by a ford and turn right into Laurel Grove. At a fork just past 'Stream Cottage' on the right go left. The track winds down to a road where turn right and after 100 yards left into Shrubbs Lane. At a crossroads turn right into The Avenue and continue ahead where the road becomes two paths and then a road again. Cross Chapel Road and continue in The Avenue. At a 'T' junction turn right past the Hare and Hounds pub.

2 One hundred yards past the Conservative Club turn right on a signed footpath. Cross a footbridge and pass Old Kiln Farm to reach the A325. Cross to the waymarked gate of the Forest Inn. Leave the garden via a pinch stile and bear slightly right across a field to a metal kissing gate. Turn left on a lane and continue under a railway arch. This section may be very wet after rain, although drainage works was being undertaken as we passed. Cross a stile on the left and follow the path beside the meandering R. Wey. Herons are usually here and in late August we were treated to a wonderful pride of goldfinches, 80 to 100 strong, feeding on the thistles. Follow the waterside path over four stiles and turn left on a lane opposite Bentley Mill.

3 In 60 yards turn left over a stile and head straight across a field towards trees. Pick up a path to the right of a shallow depression and enter woodland. Cross a stile, a railway line and another stile and continue to reach a road where you turn left. Twenty five yards past a Forestry Commission Holt Pound Inclosure entry on the left turn right on a road leading to a car park. Pass a barrier and at a junction of paths turn left past another barrier. Reach a car park and turn right with houses on your left, then at a 'T' junction turn left on a lane. In about 80 yards fork right with a field on your left. Turn left on a crossing path to recross the A325 and enter Alice Holt Forest.

4 At a fork keep left on a gravel track and keep ahead past a seat on the left. Go over a crossing track and take the next waymarked left turn to Lodge Pond. Turn right along the waterside path and, at the end of pond, right again by a boot print waymark post. Maintain direction on a gravel track and at a 'T' junction turn left. Immediately bear half right on the left hand wider grass path. Maintain direction at a junction of paths, through a car park and past St James' Church, Rowledge, on the left. At the end of Church Lane turn left passing the Cherry Tree pub on your right. The Surrey Hampshire border passes through the pub.

5 Continue to the end of the road, turn right into Fullers Road and in twenty yards fork left into Rosemary Lane. At the end of this winding lane turn left downhill, then right at the 'T' junction. Bear left into Boundstone Road and fork left at the bus stop into Brown's Walk. The path winds with fields on the left then beside a stream and widens to a track. You pass 'Stream Cottage' from the outward journey and turn left at the 'T' junction back to the pub.

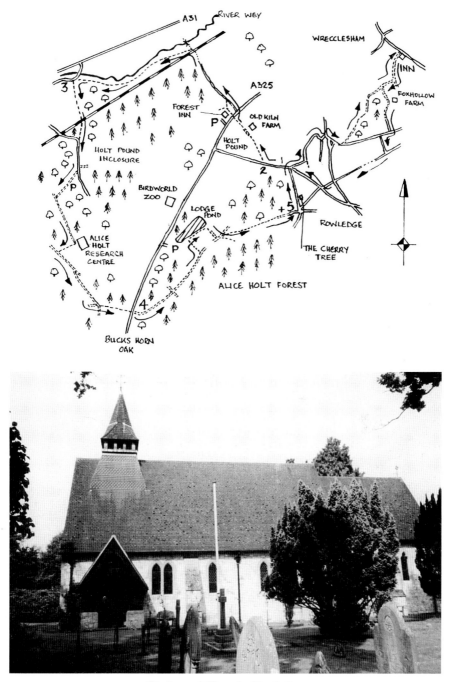

St. James' Church, Rowledge

Waverley Abbey ruin, walk 6

Bridge over River Wey by Waverley Abbey, walk 6